The Circle of Redemption: How Love, Faith, Forgiveness, and Family Came Together

Jenifer Tarver

Published by Jenifer Tarver, 2023.

THE CIRCLE OF REDEMPTION: HOW LOVE, FAITH, FORGIVENESS, AND FAMILY CAME TOGETHER

First edition. June 8, 2023.

ISBN: 979-8223225416

Written by Jenifer Tarver.

*For my beloved husband, Anthony and our children:
Brianna, Kayla, Courtney, and Anthony Jr.*

You ALL are my greatest love story.

Circle of Redemption

In the Circle of Redemption, I share the journey of how Tony and I became the unstoppable dream team that we are today. I invite you to step into my world, where I will take you on a rollercoaster ride through my highs and lows, and how I overcame every obstacle that came my way.

Our story begins as young teenagers who started a family, and over the years, have faced countless challenges and we both had to make significant sacrifices to build a life that we both wanted and deserved. But through it all, we never lost sight of what truly matters - our love for each other and our unwavering commitment to our family.

I share my secrets to making a relationship work - continuous hard work, evolution, and growth. I will tell you how I made it through the tough times, what I learned from my mistakes, and how I found the faith and strength to keep pushing forward. My journey has taught me that with love and perseverance, you can overcome any obstacle that life throws your way.

I believe that everyone has a higher power guiding them towards their destiny, and I want to help you discover yours. My story is proof that anything is possible when you have faith in yourself and a higher power. I will share how we found our own faith and used it to guide us in the right direction.

So come and join me in the Circle of Redemption, where you will find inspiration, hope, and the keys to unlocking the life that you want and deserve. Let me show you how love, faith, and perseverance can transform your life into a beautiful masterpiece.

Where It All Started: Colerain High School, January 1994

It was January 1994 when fate brought Anthony Tarver, or Tony as I affectionately call him, into my life. We were both juniors at Colerain Senior High School in Cincinnati, Ohio, and although we never shared any classes, we often crossed paths in the hallways. Little did I know, our love story was already in motion.

As a shy student, I kept to myself during school hours, but outside of school, I was bold and adventurous. I loved being outdoors, playing sports, and spending time with my guy friends from the neighborhood. Tony caught my eye with his cool demeanor, handsome looks, and infectious smile. Whenever we passed each other in the hallways, he would flash a smile at me, and my heart would skip a beat. I longed to get to know him better.

One day, fate intervened in the most unexpected way. My friend was showing a few guys a school picture of me, and Tony happened to be among them. Tony remarked that I was cute, and my friend passed the message along to me. I felt a spark of attraction, and fate was playing a hand in bringing us together.

My high school years were filled with challenges, including my parents' divorce. With my mom working long hours to make ends meet, my sisters and I often had to fend for ourselves. We were left alone a lot and had to learn how to be independent at an early age. Despite these difficulties, I took a leap of faith and wrote a letter to Tony, whom I had never spoken to before.

To my surprise, he wrote back. He mentioned that he was seeing someone, but he barely got to see her. Tony agreed to come over and hang out one weekend. As we exchanged letters, I felt a sense of excitement and anticipation growing within me. Could this be the beginning of something special?

When Tony finally came over, we hit it off immediately. We spent the day listening to music, talking, and getting to know each other. Our chemistry was undeniable, and we kissed passionately. In that moment, nothing else mattered. I was bold and carefree, unafraid to take a risk for love. I was very smitten with Tony because he was handsome, funny, and sweet.

We returned to school, and Tony surprised me with yet another letter. My heart fluttered with excitement as I read his words. I could not deny the chemistry that existed between us. However, my excitement soon turned to disappointment. Tony wrote me a letter and asked me to keep our day together a secret, as he did not want his girlfriend to find out. I felt sad and confused, but I decided to move on quickly. We did not speak to each other after that but, fate, however, had other plans.

An Unforgettable Night: A Teenage Party, April 1994

Fast forward to April 1994, my mom was heading out of town for work. She would be gone for an entire week. My sisters and I had planned a party and invited some friends over. I do not know what possessed me, but I wanted Tony to come. He still had a girlfriend, but I did not care. I could not resist the spark that I felt was still there. I scribbled a note to him, explaining that my mom was going out of town and asked him to join us. Tony wrote back, saying that he would try to make it, and we arranged a time and place to meet. I also enlisted my older sister's help in picking him up. As the day of the party approached, I could not shake the feeling that something was about to change. Would Tony show up? And if he did, what would happen between us? The anticipation was killing me.

Later that evening, Tony called me from a payphone and my sister, and I went to pick him up. We went back to my house and there were already a bunch of our friends there. The atmosphere was light and fun, and Tony's presence added a new energy to the group. As the night progressed, Tony and I found ourselves sitting next to each other, under a cozy blanket, watching a movie. The touch of his hands sent shivers down my spine, and I knew in that moment that I wanted more. We sneaked away to my room, where our passion took over. The way he looked at me, the way he touched me, made me feel alive. The chemistry between us was undeniable, and we spent the whole night together, exploring each other's bodies.

As the morning light broke through the window, we were tangled up in the sheets, not wanting to let go. We ended up skipping school that day. We spent the entire day in bed talking and making love. Then we had to face reality, and he had to leave for football practice. As we said our goodbyes, we kissed passionately and I watched him walk away, wondering if this was just a fling or something more.

After he left my house that afternoon, we did not talk to each other again. We would see each other in the hallways at school but we did not speak. I was confused and hurt because I thought we had a connection. I could not stop thinking about him though, and the magical night we had together. I knew it was foolish to believe that he might leave his girlfriend for me, but I could not help the way I felt.

A month went by, and I realized I had not gotten my period. Panic set in as I thought about the possibility of being pregnant. We did not use protection. I decided to take a pregnancy test, and my worst fears were confirmed. I was seventeen years old and at the end of my junior year of high school, I was pregnant with Tony's baby, and I barely knew him. As scared and overwhelmed as I was, there was a part of me that felt hopeful. I knew I was strong and capable of taking care of a baby. I helped my older sister take care of her son. I had to grow up quickly and make tough decisions, but I knew I could do it. I did not know how I was going to tell Tony. We were not even talking anymore. Do I write him a letter or have a friend tell him? I had no idea how Tony would react when he finds out. I held onto the hope that eventually, things would fall into place.

I Am Pregnant, Now What

When I found out that I was pregnant, fear and uncertainty overwhelmed me. Despite the difficulties ahead, I knew that I could not go through with an abortion. I have always been a strong person, and this situation was a test of my resilience. My older sister, who had a baby at sixteen while still going to school and working, inspired me with her strength. I decided to follow her example and keep the baby, determined to give my child the best life possible.

At the time, I was already working at a fast-food restaurant called White Castle since I was fifteen years old. Although it was not the ideal job, I knew I had to keep it to provide for myself and my baby. Despite the challenges of working and being pregnant, I was determined to continue my education and create a better future for my family.

Sharing my pregnancy news with my close friends and sisters was easy, but I found it difficult to tell Tony and the rest of my family. I was scared and uncertain about how they would react. Eventually, I asked a friend to break the news to Tony. As I expected, he was shocked and did not know how to respond. When he called me that night, I could sense the disbelief in his voice. He asked me what my plan was, and I told him that I had decided to keep the baby. His reaction was mixed. He confided that he was not ready to be a father, as he had a lot going on in his family life, and my pregnancy only added to his already overwhelming burden.

Tony faced significant hardships during his tenth-grade year when personal circumstances forced him to leave his mother and sister behind in another school district. Despite the challenges, he remained committed to playing football and graduating from Colerain High School. To achieve this, he persevered, and started living with a friend and their family from grades tenth to twelfth. Though he often slept on the floor, he was grateful for the roof over his head. To support himself, Tony worked at various jobs, including Burger King, Kroger, and a car wash. Eventually, his mother and sister also became homeless and were forced to live in a shelter. Nevertheless, Tony remained determined to create a better life for them all.

When I was three months pregnant, I mustered the courage to tell my mom the truth. Though I was scared of her reaction, she surprised me with her understanding and support. Having gone through a similar experience with my older sister, she knew how difficult it could be. With her by my side, I felt a sense of relief.

Walking the halls of my high school with a growing belly was a constant reminder of the challenges ahead. Tony and I barely spoke, exchanging only fleeting glances. Despite my fear and overwhelming emotions, I knew I had to stay strong for my baby. Though we were not in love, there was a spark between us that never seemed to fade. Unfortunately, we could never seem to get on the same page.

When we did speak, Tony would talk about a being together as a family, but he would often disapear to be with someone else. It would leave me feeling depressed and alone. The experience was emotionally tumultuous, and it left me feeling exhausted. Though determined to be a good mother, I couldn't help but wonder about the future of our relationship. Would we ever become a true family?

Despite the challenges I faced, I remained determined to succeed for the sake of my child. With the guidance of my counselor, I found a way to graduate early and obtain the credits I needed. I was only lacking ½ credit of English to graduate, and I was relieved to have a plan in place. It was not going to be a simple feat, as I had to balance school, tutoring, work, doctor appointments, and taking care of my growing baby. It was a demanding schedule, but I was grateful that my pregnancy was uncomplicated.

My English teacher stepped up to support me in my time of need. He offered to tutor me after school and help me to graduate early by providing me with the necessary credits I needed. During our tutoring sessions, he had me read several novels, including the book *"What to Expect When You're Expecting."* This book helped me to understand the basics of baby care and prepare for my upcoming role as a mother. He also provided me with valuable advice and even donated baby clothes to me. Having just adopted a baby girl with his wife, he knew what I was going through and was empathetic to my situation. I am incredibly grateful for his kindness and support.

Throughout my pregnancy, Tony and I talked sporadically, but he never came to any of my doctor appointments, including the one where I got my sonogram and found out I was having a baby girl. Even though I was excited and called Tony to share the news, he seemed uninterested. My emotions were all over the place as I had mixed feelings about wanting to be a family with him one minute and feeling like I could not stand him and never wanted to talk to him again the next. Despite my frustrations, I tried my best to focus on my baby and prepare for her arrival.

At eight months pregnant, Tony had still not told his mom about the baby, and he was too scared to do so. However, fate intervened when my little sister called a homeless shelter to volunteer with her classmates. As she was telling a woman that she attends Colerain High School and wants to help, the woman revealed that her son, Anthony Tarver, also goes to that school. My sister could not believe the coincidence and was eager to tell me what happened. It gave us an idea to tell Tony's mom about the pregnancy since he still had not done so. A few weeks later, my sister called the woman again and revealed that Tony got me pregnant, and I was due soon. Tony's mom was shocked and immediately called Tony. When Tony called me later that evening, he was in tears and angry that we had told his mom, but I think he was ultimately relieved to have the secret out.

With the help of my incredible friends and family, I was able to persevere through the difficulties that came with being a young, expecting mother. Their unwavering love and support fueled me with a sense of purpose and a strong determination to succeed. I was determined to be the best mother I could be to my baby girl, and I was equally committed to finishing high school, no matter the obstacles. Even though Tony was not fully invested in fatherhood, I was determined to create a bright future for my child and myself. Though the road ahead was daunting, I knew I possessed the resilience and strength to face it head on with courage and determination.

On January 20, 1995, which was coincidentally my eighteenth birthday, the first semester ended, marking the completion of my tutoring, and earning the English credit required for early graduation. Thanks to my unwavering dedication and effort, I was able to finish all my credits in time, which meant that I did not have to attend the second semester. It was a proud moment for me, and it served as a testament to the fact that perseverance and hard work can truly pay off. This experience was a reminder that even in the darkest moments, there is always a glimmer of hope and that there is light at the end of the tunnel.

Brianna Nicole: January 25, 1995

On a chilly January afternoon in 1995, just five days after my eighteenth birthday, I felt a sharp pain in my lower abdomen. I knew immediately that I was going into labor. After packing a bag with some essentials, my family and I rushed to the hospital. My little sister, who was still in school, came along with us, her eyes wide with excitement.

As we checked in at the hospital, my nerves were on edge. I had never experienced anything like this before, and I feared what was to come. I also felt a sense of excitement and anticipation, knowing that I was about to meet my first child.

Meanwhile, Tony was still at school, completely unaware of what was happening. I had my sister tell him that I was in labor. While I was in the hospital, Tony called me. He had just arrived home from school, and when he heard I was in labor, he immediately said he was going to try to find a ride to come to the hospital and see me.

My mother, a constant source of strength and support, was by my side throughout the entire labor. As the contractions grew more intense, she tirelessly rubbed my lower back, trying to ease the pain. I clung to her hand, squeezing it tightly with each wave of discomfort that washed over me.

Despite my best efforts, my daughter did not seem to want to come out. The pushing seemed endless, and I grew increasingly frustrated and exhausted. It was not until the doctor brought out the forceps that progress was finally made. Even then, it was not easy, and I remember feeling a sharp pain as the forceps were applied.

Finally, after what felt like an eternity, my baby girl was born. I remember the moment vividly: the doctor lifted her up and placed her on my chest, and I felt an overwhelming sense of love and joy. She was perfect, with a head full of dark hair and a pair of bright, curious eyes that seemed to take in everything around her.

As I held her close, I could not believe that I was a mother. All the challenges I had faced up to this point - the struggles, the sacrifices, the doubts - suddenly seemed so small in comparison to the miracle that had just occurred. In that moment, I knew that everything was worth it.

As I held my newborn daughter in my arms, I felt an indescribable mix of emotions - joy, wonder, gratitude, and a love so fierce it took my breath away. Everything else in the world seemed to fade away, leaving only the two of us in a cocoon of warmth and affection.

It was both surreal and humorous to me that the father of my child, Tony, was not able to make it to the hospital in time for the birth. He did not have a ride. I felt extremely disappointed and hurt but I could not hold a grudge against him. I knew that he was just as eager to meet our daughter as I was, and circumstances beyond his control had kept him away. When he finally did arrive at my house two days later, his face was filled with both excitement and anxiety.

As he held our daughter for the first time, I saw a look of wonder and awe in his eyes that mirrored my own. Even though we were young and inexperienced, we both knew that we were in this together - that we would face all the challenges of parenthood as a team, no matter what the future held.

Bringing my newborn daughter Brianna home was an experience unlike any other. I was filled with a sense of excitement and nervousness as I embarked on my journey as a new mom. The thought of caring for another life was intimidating, but I knew that I had the support of my family to help me through the challenges ahead.

Despite the endless sleepless nights and the constant demands of taking care of a newborn, I found that caring for Brianna came naturally to me. I relished every moment with her, from the gentle caress of her tiny hand to the sweet sound of her coos and gurgles.

As I settled into my new role as a mother, Tony came over frequently. The love and joy in his eyes were palpable as he held Brianna. He could not stop marveling at her beauty, and I could see the pride and wonder in his face as he looked at her.

It was clear to me that he was just as smitten with Brianna as I was. As we looked at our daughter together, I felt a sense of deep contentment and happiness that filled me with a sense of hope for the future. Despite all the challenges that lay ahead, I knew that we would face them together, as a family.

When Brianna was just six weeks old, I made the decision to return to work at White Castle. It was not easy, but I knew that I had to provide for my daughter and myself, and that meant making some sacrifices.

To make it work, I opted for the night shift from 11:00pm-7:00am, which meant that I would be away from Brianna during her most vulnerable hours. I did not have much of a choice - I needed to earn a living, and the night shift offered me a chance to be with her during the day.

I was incredibly fortunate to have my mother by my side during this challenging time. She offered to watch over Brianna at night while I was at work, and I will always be grateful for her support. Even with her help, it was a difficult period for me. I had to stay up during the day to take care of Brianna, and then work through the night when I should have been sleeping. It was a constant cycle of exhaustion, and I often felt like I was running on fumes.

Despite the challenges, I persevered. I slept when Brianna did and took every opportunity to rest when I could. I knew that being a mother meant making sacrifices, and I was willing to do whatever it took to provide for my daughter and myself. Looking back, it was a tough time, but it taught me the importance of hard work and dedication, and it gave me the strength to face the challenges of motherhood head-on.

Returning home from my night shifts was always a bittersweet experience. On the one hand, I was exhausted and eager to rest. But on the other, I was greeted by my little bundle of joy, who was always wide awake and ready to play.

Brianna's infectious laughter and cute little smile brought happiness to everyone around her. People could not help but stop and stare at her. She looked like a little baby doll, with rosy cheeks and bright, curious eyes that seemed to take in everything around her. Her head full of hair was the envy of many - even strangers on the street would stop to compliment her on her luscious locks.

I felt proud to be her mother, not just because of her adorable looks, but because of the joy and light she brought into my life. Despite the challenges and the exhaustion, being a mother was the greatest thing that had ever happened to me. Every time Brianna looked up at me with those big, beautiful brown eyes, I felt a surge of love and warmth that I had never experienced before.

Looking back on those early days, I realize now that Brianna was more than just my baby - she was a source of strength and inspiration for me. Her resilience and her boundless energy reminded me that no matter how hard things might seem, there was always a reason to keep going. I knew that if I had her by my side, I could face any challenge that life might throw my way.

Could We Be a Family

After Brianna was born, Tony stepped up in a big way. He was incredibly involved in our lives, coming over to my house after school and calling me frequently to check in. It was like we were a picture-perfect family, and I could not have been happier.

Tony was always happy to help in any way he could. He would bring over diapers and formula when we needed them, and he was never too busy to lend a hand with whatever was required. Watching him with Brianna, I felt my heart swell with pride and joy. He was a natural father, and I could see how much he loved our daughter.

As we spent more time together, Tony and I were getting to know each other in a whole new way. We talked about our hopes and dreams for the future, and we shared our thoughts on parenting and what it meant to raise a child. I was amazed at how much we had in common, and how comfortable we were with each other.

I could not believe how much my life had changed since Brianna was born. It was like everything I had ever wanted was right in front of me. I had a beautiful daughter, a supportive family, and a partner who loved me and wanted to be a part of our lives. The challenges of being a new mother were still there, but somehow, they seemed easier to face when I had Tony by my side. Together, we were building a family that I always dreamed of.

Life is unpredictable and things never stayed perfect for too long. Just when I thought everything was going smoothly, Tony would disappear for weeks without any explanation. It was like he had vanished into thin air, leaving me to wonder what had happened. His frequent vanishing acts left me wondering where he was and what he was up to. One moment, he wanted to be a part of our daughter's life, and the next moment, he was nowhere to be found, living his own life without a care in the world.

His absence was a constant reminder that I was on my own to take care of Brianna. It was exhausting and overwhelming, and I often found myself feeling lost and alone. All I ever wanted was to have a happy family with Tony, but his inconsistencies and unexplained absences shattered that dream into pieces. Despite the heartbreak and confusion, I remained resilient and strong for my daughter. I knew I had to put her first and keep pushing forward, no matter how difficult it may be. The bond between Brianna and me was unbreakable, and she was the reason I never gave up hope for a brighter future.

As the weeks turned into months, I found myself becoming more and more resilient. I started to realize that I was capable of taking care of Brianna on my own, without Tony's help. I juggled work and responsibilities to make sure that Brianna had everything she needed. As a result, I became more independent and self-sufficient, learning to rely on my own strength and determination to keep going.

Despite the challenges, Brianna continued to be my source of joy and inspiration. Her infectious laughter and boundless energy lifted my spirits and kept me going through the darkest of times. Through it all, I realized that I was creating a life for her that was full of love, happiness, and endless possibilities.

Graduating High School: May 1995

Graduation day was the pinnacle of everything I had worked for, and I could not wait to share it with Tony and my classmates. Despite the challenges I had faced as a young, pregnant mother, I was able to graduate with honors while working a part-time job at White Castle. Looking back, I realized how much I had overcame and how proud I was of myself for never giving up. It was an achievement I could share with my daughter, who had inspired me to keep going no matter how hard things got. Though my relationship with Tony may not have been the fairy tale romance I had dreamed of, I had found a new kind of love through my daughter, and my determination had paid off in the end.

As I navigated through the complexities of motherhood and high school, Tony remained an enigma. Despite the hurdles we had overcome together, it felt like he was slipping away. We barely spoke, and our relationship was strained. I knew that Tony had his own struggles, especially with his family situation, but I could not help feeling frustrated and hurt by his distance.

As we graduated with our massive class of nearly nine hundred students, I couldn't help but feel a twinge of disappointment. Even in a sea of people, I spotted Tony's beaming smile, and I longed to congratulate him on his achievement. As much as I wanted to approach him, something held me back, and we remained strangers in a crowd. To add to my sadness, Tony did not even acknowledge Brianna's presence that night, and I could not understand why he was shutting us out. It seemed like he would disappear for weeks, leaving us in the dark, and then reappear as if nothing had happened. The uncertainty was taking its toll on me.

The uncertainty of our future weighed heavy on my mind as I held my diploma. I felt a sense of pride in my achievement, but also a sense of fear about what was to come. I did not have any desire to go to college. I also did not think that was an option because I had to work to make money to provide for my daughter.

As for Tony, his plans remained a mystery. It seemed like he was content with just taking life as it came, while I was busy planning for the future. It was frustrating because I wanted him to be a part of our lives, but I could not depend on him to be there all the time.

The feeling of accomplishment after graduation was exhilarating, but it was also a reminder of the challenges ahead. The reality of being a single mother with no clear plan for the future was daunting, but I refused to let fear consume me. I knew that I had to keep pushing forward for the sake of my daughter. I refused to let anything hold me back. I wanted to provide her with a stable and happy life, even if it meant sacrificing my own dreams and desires. Instead, I chose to embrace the unpredictable nature of life and find joy in the unexpected. I learned to laugh at the absurdity of it all, and that gave me the strength to keep pushing forward. I was determined to make the best of every situation, no matter how challenging it may be.

What's Next for Us

It was the summer of 1996, and my family was packing up our childhood home in Cincinnati, Ohio. My mom, a native of Kansas City, MO, was eager to move back to her hometown after my parents' divorce and our high school graduations. But for me, the thought of leaving behind everything I knew and loved in Cincinnati was almost too much to bear. The hardest part, leaving behind my child's father, with whom I still wanted to be a family with.

As my family prepared to move to Kansas City, I knew deep down that I could not leave Cincinnati. This was my home, the place where I had grown up and made countless memories. With no house and no support system in place, it seemed impossible to stay. That is, until my aunt and uncle stepped in.

With open hearts and arms, they welcomed me into their home and provided a safe haven during a difficult time. They understood the challenges I was facing and offered their unwavering support. Thanks to them, I was able to continue working my night shift job, despite not having a license or car. Every day, they drove me back and forth to work, a big and meaningful gesture that made a world of difference to me. Their kindness gave me the strength to keep going, to believe that I could make it on my own in this city that I loved so much. For that, I will always be grateful.

My aunt and uncle were there for me every step of the way, offering their love and support in ways that went above and beyond. As time went on, my uncle became not just a mentor, but a father figure to me.

He saw potential in me that I did not even know existed, and he was determined to help me succeed. One day, he offered to teach me how to drive. When my uncle offered to teach me how to drive, I was hesitant at first. I was nineteen years old and had never gotten my license, thanks to a traumatic experience that had left me terrified of being behind the wheel.

Years earlier, when I was just sixteen, my aunt and uncle had offered to let me practice driving when they got off work. My cousin and I took their car out one afternoon, and I was slowly gaining confidence as we made our way down the road. But then, disaster struck. As I tried to pull into a friend's driveway, I panicked and hit the gas instead of the brakes, slamming into a tree and totaling my aunt's car.

My cousin and I were both okay, thankfully, but we knew that we had to cover up what had happened. So, we concocted a lie: she would take the blame for the accident, telling our aunt and uncle that she had been driving instead of me. I was grateful beyond words, knowing that my cousin had saved me from the consequences of my mistake.

The experience left me shaken and scared, and I did not want to get behind the wheel again. It was not until my uncle offered to teach me again how to drive that I began to see the possibility of a different future, one where I could conquer my fears and gain the freedom that comes with a driver's license. It was a journey that would take time and effort, but I knew that with my uncle's patience and guidance, I could make it happen.

Finally, after years of fear and uncertainty, I did it. I got my driver's license, and I felt like I was on top of the world. I had come so far from that terrified sixteen-year-old who had crashed her aunt's car, and I was proud of myself for facing my fears and persevering.

None of it would have been possible without my uncle. He had taken the time to teach me how to drive, step by step, always patient and kind even when I made mistakes or got frustrated. He had been a mentor and a father figure to me, guiding me through some of the toughest times of my life and helping me see the light at the end of the tunnel.

Then, another life-changing moment: my uncle helped me purchase my very own car. I will never forget the feeling of sitting behind the wheel for the first time, the wind in my hair and a sense of freedom and possibility at my fingertips. It was a moment that symbolized so much more than just a new vehicle; it represented the power of love and support, and the knowledge that with the right people by your side, anything is possible.

I knew then that I would always be indebted to my uncle, and that I would never forget the impact he had on my life. He taught me to believe in myself, to trust in my own abilities, and to never give up, no matter how hard the challenge. And for that, I will be forever grateful.

Even though everything was going well for me and Brianna, there was still a part of me that longed for Tony. I knew he was going through some tough times, but my love for him just kept growing stronger. He was living in the projects in Covington, Kentucky with his mom and sister. He started selling drugs and using them, but I just could not shake the feeling that he was the one for me.

After high school, Tony started hanging out with the wrong crowd and got mixed up in drugs. I was worried about him and his well-being. It just was not the Tony I knew. He became paranoid and was not himself. We still talked and saw each other from time to time, and our chemistry was undeniable. It was like a magnet pulling us together. I know some people might call me stupid or idiotic for sticking with him, but my heart felt differently.

Even though he had other girlfriends and we only saw each other from time to time, our attraction was indisputable and every time we saw each other, we would end up having sex. Despite the difficulties in our relationship, I remained hopeful that we would one day be together as a family.

Looking back, I sometimes wonder if I was just a naive girl, foolishly holding onto a dream that would never come true. At the time, I could not help the way I felt. My love for Tony was deep and real, and I could not imagine my life without him. Little did I know that our journey together was far from over, and that we still had many twists and turns ahead.

Pregnancy #2

As I stared at the positive pregnancy test, a sense of dread washed over me. Here I was, only nineteen years old, and pregnant again. How could I let this happen again? I felt lost and overwhelmed, unsure of what to do next. Tony and I were not even together at the time and barely speaking. My mind raced with all sorts of thoughts and questions. How was I going to take care of two children on my own? What was my family going to say? I felt confused and scared. Being a young, single mother of two was not what I had planned for my life. I did not know if I was ready for another child.

As I contemplated my next steps, I realized that I had a choice to make. I could either let fear and doubt consume me, or I could rise above my circumstances and embrace the future with open arms. In that moment, I chose to believe in myself and my ability to overcome any obstacle. The next step was to tell Tony.

As I gathered the courage to tell Tony, my heart felt heavy with anxiety. Would he even care? Would he be angry or disappointed? These thoughts plagued my mind as I picked up the phone and dialed his number. When he answered, I took a deep breath and blurted out the news. There was a long pause on the other end of the line before he finally spoke. He was shocked and unsure of what to say, but eventually, he came around and promised to support me and our children.

Despite Tony's promise, I still had doubts and fears. How would we make this work? Would Tony stick around and be a dependable partner and father? How would we provide for our growing family? I was determined to make it work, with the support of my family and Tony.

Receiving Tony's assurance was a huge relief for me, but I knew that words alone were not enough. However, as time went on, Tony's actions proved that he was indeed committed to being a part of our lives. He made an effort to spend time with me, Brianna, and the growing baby inside me. He was always there to lend a helping hand. I was grateful for the support he provided.

During the pregnancy, Tony proved his commitment to our family by being present for every step of the journey. He would accompany me to all my doctor's appointments and ultrasounds, holding my hand and offering words of encouragement. He would often rub my belly and talk to our unborn baby, showing his love and excitement for the new addition to our family. It was like he had transformed into a different person, one who was responsible and caring. Seeing him take on these new roles was both surprising and comforting, and I felt grateful to have him by my side. Tony had become the man I always dreamed of, and I could not wait to start our new life together as a family.

The thought of our future together filled us both with a sense of possibility and adventure. Tony was determined to provide for us, so he took on multiple jobs to support our growing family. I was still living with my aunt and uncle and working night shift. We even talked about moving in together and getting married, which only added to the thrill of building a life together. The love we shared was palpable, and it seemed like anything was possible with Tony by my side.

Despite the challenges that lay ahead, I knew that Tony and I would face them together. Looking back, I realized that honesty and communication were key to our success. It was not always easy, but we were committed to making things work. We talked about everything, from our fears and doubts to our hopes and dreams. We made plans together and supported each other every step of the way.

Through it all, our love continued to grow. We learned to lean on each other and trust in our love. We faced financial struggles, parenting challenges, and personal hardships, but we never lost sight of our love for each other. We were determined to build a life together, and nothing could stand in our way.

Our love story was just beginning, and I could not wait to see where it would take us. I knew that we had a bright future ahead of us, filled with endless possibilities.

Kayla Renee: March 19, 1997

In December 1996, I took a leap of faith and moved out of my aunt and uncle's house to live in the projects with Tony's family. It was a significant step for me as I had grown up in a middle-class environment, and the projects were an entirely different world. I was willing to take that risk for Tony, for us, for our future together. Despite the challenges of living in an unfamiliar place with a young child, I was content because I was with the man I loved. It felt like we were building a life together, brick by brick, and I was excited to see where it would take us.

In March 1997, Tony and I were thrilled to move into our own place in the same projects. We did not have much to furnish our new home, but we were filled with hope and excitement for the future. As we settled into our new space, we began to build a home filled with love and warmth. We decorated with second-hand furniture and handmade crafts. It was not much, but it was ours, and we were proud of it. Every day felt like a new adventure, as we learned how to navigate life as young parents. Despite the challenges, we were happy and content, knowing that we were building a life together.

The financial strain on our little family was starting to take its toll. I stopped making payments on my car, and it was not long before the repo man came knocking. It happened one night while I was working the night shift. My car was gone, and I felt embarrassed and worried. I lived forty-five minutes away from our new place, and Tony did not have a car. With our baby due in just a few weeks, I was incredibly stressed out, trying to first figure out how to get home and how we would manage without a car.

As I woke up in the early hours of March 19, 1997, I felt a sudden discomfort in my lower abdomen. It was a feeling that I had become familiar with during my pregnancy. I realized that my water broke. I immediately woke up Tony and called my older sister, who lived over an hour away, to give us a ride to the hospital since we did not have a car. She rushed over and drove us to the hospital while Brianna stayed with her.

I remember feeling a mix of excitement and nerves as we arrived at the hospital. This was going to be our second child, and while I had an easy pregnancy, I could not help but feel anxious about the labor and delivery process. Tony held my hand as we made our way to the maternity ward, and I was greeted by a team of kind and experienced nurses who helped me get settled in.

The labor was not too bad, and I managed to get through it without any major complications. As I pushed through the final stages, I could feel the adrenaline pumping through my body. Then, finally, our little bundle of joy arrived. The nurses cleaned up our baby and placed her in my arms. Tony and I were overjoyed as we looked down at our newborn daughter. She was beautiful. She had a head full of hair but not as much as Brianna did. She also had beautiful green eyes like mine. She was perfect.

I remember feeling a sense of pride as I held her in my arms, knowing that we had created this beautiful life together. It was a moment of pure happiness, and for a brief moment, all of our worries about money and the challenges of raising a family melted away. We had brought another baby into this world, and that was all that mattered in that moment.

Tony's transformation into a devoted father was nothing short of remarkable. Despite his past involvement in selling drugs, he had a newfound sense of determination to do right by our family. He embraced fatherhood with open arms, taking care of our two girls with unwavering devotion. He changed diapers, helped with feeding, and even stayed up late at night to rock our newborn back to sleep. Watching him step up and take responsibility filled me with inspiration and hope for our future together as a family.

Tony's commitment to being present for our family was evident in his actions. He made sure that our girls were well-fed, clothed, and had a roof over their heads. I remember feeling overwhelmed with gratitude and love for this man who had transformed into such an incredible partner and father. It was clear that he was committed to being the best father and partner he could be. I felt grateful every day for the family we had built together.

So, after my six weeks of maternity leave were up, I had to go back to work. But I had a problem - I did not have a car to get me there. I could not afford to buy a new one, so I called up my dad and asked if he could help me out. He came through for me and bought me a $3000 car. It was not the fanciest car, but it was dependable and got me where I needed to go. I was so grateful for his help. With my new wheels, I went back to working the night shift at White Castle while Tony took care of our kids at home.

As we settled into our new routine, I could not help but feel grateful for Tony's unwavering support. Even though I was exhausted all the time, he was always there to lend a helping hand. Our house in the projects may not have been the most glamorous place to call home, but it was filled with so much love and laughter that it felt like a palace to us. I remember the way Tony would make us all laugh with his silly jokes and impressions, and how he would spend hours playing with our girls and teaching them new things. Despite our struggles, we were building a life together that was rich in joy and contentment. Looking back, I am amazed at how far we have come and how much we have accomplished as a family. It wasn't always easy, but with Tony by my side, I knew we could overcome any obstacle.

Rollercoaster Ride

Everything was going great with Tony, until the day he decided to stop working and become a full-time dad. I was proud of him for stepping up and taking care of our daughters, but things started to change as time went on. He started smoking weed more frequently, and I noticed he seemed unhappy about not having a job or money. We began to argue, and our fights escalated to screaming matches. It was a challenging time for our relationship, and I felt like we were at a crossroads. Would we be able to work through this challenging period, or would it tear us apart? Despite the struggles, I still loved Tony and believed that we could find a way to overcome our issues together.

Kicking Tony out of the house and watching him go stay at his mom's house down the street was becoming a familiar routine. It became a regular occurrence. It was hard to keep track of where he was and what he was doing. What made it worse was when he started seeing his ex-girlfriends again, which left me feeling hurt and confused. The constant cycle of arguing, kicking him out, and then taking him back was emotionally draining. I did not know if our relationship was going to survive this.

As I turned onto our street after a long night shift at White Castle, I felt a sinking feeling in my chest when I saw Tony's ex-girlfriend's car parked outside his mother's house. The fear and pain in my heart were so intense that it was like a knife piercing through my soul. This was the first time I had seen it so clearly in my face, and it was soul crushing. For months, I had been struggling with Tony's constant back-and-forth between me, and it had taken a serious toll on our relationship. This was the moment of truth that I had been dreading, and I knew I had to confront him.

I stormed to his mom's front door and banged on it with all my might, calling out for Tony and his ex-girlfriend, but there was no answer. I felt like I was being played, like I was not good enough for him, and the pain was too much to bear. I stumbled back to my house and collapsed on the floor, crying my eyes out and asking God for help. I told God that I could not take the back and forth anymore, and that my heart could not manage the pain. I begged for a sign and asked if Tony was really the one for me. In my despair, I begged for a sign, a clear indication of whether Tony was truly the right person for me or not.

In that moment of utter desperation, I heard a voice, like an angel's whisper, telling me that Tony was the one I was meant to be with, and that I should not give up. The voice was like a soothing balm to my wounded heart, and it gave me the answers I desperately needed. In that moment I picked myself off the ground and decided to fight for our love.

Despite my best efforts, it was clear that Tony was not willing to work on our relationship. I felt completely heartbroken and desperate, doing anything I could to try and make him stay. I wanted to become the perfect person for him and make our relationship work. The pain of rejection and heartbreak was almost too much to bear. Looking back, I cringe at how vulnerable and helpless I felt in those moments. But then, something inside me shifted. I realized that I had been putting all my energy into trying to please someone else, instead of focusing on my own growth and happiness.

Then I remembered the voice I had heard, telling me not to give up on him. I realized that I had to focus on being the best version of myself, not just for Tony, but for me and our daughters. Eventually, Tony did come back, but things were different this time. He saw the changes I had made and was impressed by my newfound confidence and drive. We both knew that we still had work to do on our relationship, but I was no longer willing to sacrifice my own happiness for his. Through hard work, love, and determination, we were able to rebuild our relationship and create a stronger, healthier, and happier family.

Happily, Ever After

About eight months after Kayla was born, my life took a major turn. I made the bold decision to leave my job at White Castle, where I had been working for almost five years, and start a new career at a law firm in downtown Cincinnati. The job paid me what I deserved, and it was a day shift position, which meant I could spend more time with my family and finally get enough sleep. It was a real success for me, even though I started out as a file clerk.

The change in my life also marked a turning point in my relationship with Tony. We were working hard to make our relationship work again, and he was thrilled about my new job. We started talking about our future together, planning our wedding, and dreaming of a life filled with love and happiness. We were deeply in love, and nothing could stop us. Every moment with him felt like a dream come true, and I could not imagine spending my life with anyone else.

As I settled into my new job, I began to realize that my hard work was paying off. I enjoyed working at the law firm, and I was proud of the progress I was making in my career. Tony was my biggest supporter, and his encouragement gave me the confidence to keep pushing forward. Together, we were building a life that was filled with promise and hope. Our future was bright, and we were ready to embrace it with open hearts and open minds.

With Tony back to work, it felt like we were both moving in the right direction. He seemed happier and more content, and I was thrilled to see him in a better place. We found a babysitter to take care of our kids while we were at work, and it was a great relief to know they were in good hands. Working the day shift was a game-changer for us, too. We were finally able to spend more time together as a family, and it felt like we were hitting our stride.

As I settled into my new job at the law firm, I felt increasingly grateful for the positive changes in our lives. Tony and I were able to support each other in ways we never had before, and it was clear that we were both committed to making our relationship work. We were building a foundation for our future, and it felt solid and strong.

When I woke up on Christmas morning in 1997, I felt a surge of excitement and anticipation. It was my favorite holiday of the year, and I was thrilled to be celebrating it with my family. As I watched Brianna open her presents with joy and wonder, I could not help but feel like a kid again myself. Christmas always held a special place in my heart, and this year was no exception.

As I looked around at my family, I felt overwhelmed with gratitude. My grandma had always been the heart and soul of our Christmas celebrations, and even though she was no longer with us, her spirit lived on in the love and warmth we shared. Kayla, too young to understand what was going on, was content to watch her big sister play with her new toys. I felt blessed to have such a loving family, and I knew that this was a special holiday that I would always cherish.

For me, Christmas was more than just a holiday. It was a time to reflect on all the special memories and moments that had shaped my life. It was a time to connect with my family and friends and to share in the joy and wonder of the season.

As we finished opening our Christmas presents, I noticed that Tony had a mischievous glint in his eye. I could not quite figure out what he was up to, but I didn't dwell on it for too long. Then, he surprised me with another present - a small box with a cheap-looking ring inside. I was puzzled and unsure of what to think, and my face must have given away my confusion. He asked me if I liked the ring, and I sat in silence for a moment before finally admitting that I did not.

Then, Tony pulled out the real ring, and suddenly everything became clear. He got down on one knee in front of our little family, and my heart raced with anticipation. Tears streamed down my face as he asked me to marry him, and I could hardly contain my joy and excitement. It was a moment that I would never forget, a moment that marked the beginning of our forever.

I said yes, of course, filled with love and gratitude for this man who had just given me the most beautiful gift of all. Our love had been through its ups and downs, but in that moment, I knew that we were meant to be together. As I looked around at our little family, I felt more blessed than ever. This was the start of a new chapter in our lives, a chapter filled with love, commitment, and endless possibilities.

Looking back on that Christmas day, I can hardly believe how far we have come. Tony and I have been through so much together, but our love has only grown stronger with each passing year. We have faced our fair share of challenges, but we've also experienced moments of pure joy and happiness. That Christmas, with its surprise proposal and overflowing love, will always hold a special place in my heart.

Tony's proposal was everything I had ever wanted - and more. He knew how much I loved Christmas, and he made it even more special by choosing that day to pop the question. I was over the moon with happiness and excitement.

I could not help but laugh at his little joke with the fake ring - Tony had always had a great sense of humor, and he knew exactly how to make me smile. It was the perfect proposal in every way, and I knew that I was finally getting my happily ever after.

Looking back on that moment now, I still feel a warm glow in my heart. Tony and I have been through so much together, but that moment of pure love and happiness will always be a cherished memory. I knew then that I had found my soulmate, and that we were meant to spend the rest of our lives together.

Despite the joy and excitement of our engagement, I could not help but feel a sense of unease. Our relationship had always been tumultuous, with difficulties that left me feeling uncertain about our future. We've never had many good role models for healthy relationships expect my aunt and uncle, and we had to learn how to make it work on our own.

We both had our flaws and struggles. Our arguments could turn ugly, with hurtful words and actions on both sides. I would lose my temper and lash out at Tony, throwing my ring at him and cursing him out. He, in turn, would retreat into silence and withdraw from the conversation. We did not have effective communication skills, and it made it difficult to resolve our issues.

Tony was also dealing with his own challenges. He had always dreamed of having a successful career and providing for our family, but he was stuck in dead-end jobs that left him feeling frustrated and unfulfilled. He did not want to rely on me for financial support - he wanted to be the one to provide everything for us. It was a noble goal, but it also added to the stress and tension in our relationship.

As Tony and I faced each new challenge, doubts would inevitably creep in. We were two imperfect people with no model of a healthy relationship to follow, and it often felt like everything was stacked against us. But in moments of clarity, I would remember the love we shared. I would think back to the way his eyes sparkled with hope for our future together when he proposed on Christmas morning, or the small moments of joy we shared - a tender kiss, a shared laugh, a comforting hug. In those moments, I knew that our love was real and worth fighting for. Despite our flaws and difficulties, we were determined to create something beautiful together. And so, we continued to work through our struggles, never giving up on each other and overcoming whatever obstacles came our way.

United States Marine Corps

Tony had always felt like he was lacking purpose in his life. Despite his best efforts to work hard and provide for our family, he could not shake the feeling that there was something missing. Then, one day, he dropped a bombshell that would change our lives forever: he was going to join the United States Marines. I was completely taken aback - I had never heard Tony express any interest in the military before. As he explained his decision to me, I could see the fire in his eyes and hear the determination in his voice. He had talked to a recruiter after high school but had to wait because of his drug use. He was tired of feeling like he was not living up to his potential and saw the Marines as an opportunity to find belonging and purpose.

As Tony made the life-changing decision to join the United States Marines, my heart was filled with a mix of emotions. On one hand, I was incredibly proud of him for taking control of his life and pursuing a lifelong dream. But on the other hand, I could not ignore the wave of fear and uncertainty that hit me hard. We both knew that his decision would come with extended periods of separation, uncertainty, and potential danger. It was a lot to process, but as we talked it over, we both knew that we were in this together.

We were a team, and we would do whatever it took to support each other through this journey. As I thought more about it, I began to realize that this could also be a turning point for our family. Yes, there would be challenges, but there would also be opportunities for financial stability, travel, and connection with a community of like-minded individuals. I could not help feeling a little glimmer of hope amidst all the confusion.

As a military spouse, I knew that I would have to be resilient and adaptable to whatever challenges came our way. I was confident that with Tony by my side, we could build a strong and supportive life together, no matter where our journey took us. This was our chance to create something meaningful and impactful, not just for ourselves but for our family and country as well.

As we set out on this journey, we did so with the knowledge that we were not alone. We had the support of our family, friends, and the wider military community. Most importantly, we had each other. The road ahead would be tough, but we were both ready to face it head-on. We believed that this journey would ultimately be worth it, and we were willing to make the sacrifices necessary to support Tony's service to our country.

As Tony's departure date drew closer, a whirlwind of emotions overtook me. I was filled with an overwhelming sense of sadness, knowing that I would have to spend the next three months without him by my side. The thought of being alone was daunting, and I worried about how I would manage everything on my own. As I looked at Tony, I could see the excitement and determination in his eyes, and I felt an immense sense of pride welling up inside me. He was embarking on a new chapter in his life, pursuing something he felt passionate about, and I knew he had the potential to make an outstanding Marine. I promised him that I would hold down the fort and be his support system back at home, no matter how tough things got.

The day of Tony's departure had finally arrived, and as we packed his bags and said our goodbyes, my heart was filled with a mix of emotions. I felt sadness because I would miss him dearly during the three months of boot camp ahead of him. I also felt fear because I did not know how I would manage everything on my own. Despite all that, I felt an overwhelming sense of admiration and pride for Tony.

Watching him take this bold step towards his dream of becoming a Marine was truly inspiring. I knew that it was not an easy decision to make, but he had the courage and determination to pursue what he felt enthusiastic about. As he boarded the bus to take him to boot camp, my heart swelled with both pride and sadness.

It was tough to see him go, but I knew that this journey would only make us stronger. I promised myself to be strong and supportive throughout his training and beyond. I was determined to make the most of the next three months, to focus on our family, and to prepare for his return as a proud Marine. With that thought in mind, I felt a renewed sense of hope and determination to face the challenges that lay ahead.

Pregnancy #3

As I sat in my bedroom staring at the positive pregnancy test, my mind was in a frenzy. How could this be happening now? Tony was only a month into boot camp, and I was already struggling to manage our two young children on my own. The thought of a third child seemed overwhelming and affording daycare or a babysitter for three kids seemed impossible. I knew I needed to tell Tony, but the only way to communicate was through letters, and it would take days or even weeks for him to receive my message.

As the days passed, my anxiety grew. I tried to keep myself busy with the kids and household chores, but my mind kept wandering to the thought of being a mother of three at such a youthful age of twenty-one. I could not help but feel like I was in this alone. Even though I had a supportive family, I missed Tony's strength and comfort. His absence made me feel vulnerable and helpless.

When I finally received a letter from Tony, my heart skipped a beat. I eagerly tore open the envelope, hoping to find words of comfort and assurance. Instead, I read about the harsh realities of boot camp and the grueling physical and mental challenges he was facing. I knew I had to tell him about the pregnancy, but I also did not want to add any stress or worry to his already heavy burden.

Eventually, I mustered up the courage to write to him about the pregnancy. My heart felt heavy with worry and doubt. I had missed my period, and the thought of being pregnant again was overwhelming. To make matters worse, Tony was not here to help me through it. I longed for his embrace, his strength, his love.

As I put pen to paper, I found myself pouring out my heart to Tony, sharing my deepest fears and doubts. I told him how scared I was about the future and how much I missed him. I sent the letter, and then the waiting game began.

Days went by, and I waited anxiously for a reply. Every day felt like an eternity, as I checked the mailbox for any word from Tony. I started to worry that maybe he didn't want a third child, or that he was disappointed. I had no idea what he was thinking. Finally, his letter arrived, and my heart leaped with joy. In it, he shared his own worries and fears about being away from us and missing our family's milestones.

He went on to say that he had tried to leave boot camp to come home to be with me, but the drill instructor talked him out of it. Despite the setback, Tony's words were a balm to my worried soul. He reminded me that we were in this together and that he was fighting for a better life for us. His love for me and our family inspired me to keep going, to keep believing that we could overcome any obstacle together.

His letter gave me hope and the strength to face whatever challenges lay ahead. I knew that our journey would be tough, but with Tony by my side, I felt like we could conquer anything.

Spending the pregnancy alone without Tony was hard. I felt like I was reliving the same situation that I had experienced with Brianna all over again. It was tough to carry the weight of my family on my shoulders, but I knew deep down that Tony's sacrifice would pay off. Despite feeling lonely, I was grateful for the support of my family, who stepped in to help with Brianna and Kayla whenever they could.

Working long hours on my feet while pregnant was exhausting, but I had no choice but to keep pushing forward. Every day felt like a marathon, and I struggled to find moments to rest. Going to doctor's appointments alone was also hard, but I tried to remind myself that it was just another hurdle to overcome.

When it was time for my sonogram, Tony and I were both hoping for a boy, but we were surprised to learn that we were having another girl. It was bittersweet news, but we were overjoyed to know that our family was growing. I was due around Christmas time, and the thought of having a new addition to our family during the most magical time of the year filled me with happiness. Despite the challenges ahead, the prospect of holding our new baby girl in our arms gave me the strength to keep going.

During those long weeks, I stayed busy taking care of our two daughters and preparing for the new baby's arrival. The pregnancy was tough, but I was thrilled to be bringing another child into our family. The anticipation of seeing Tony again made the days pass more quickly.

Boot Camp Graduation: June 19, 1998

Finally, the day arrived. I packed up the car with a map, snacks, and toys for the kids, and we set off on our journey to Parris Island. The long ten-hour drive from Covington, KY to Parris Island, SC was arduous and challenging, especially with two young children in tow. Brianna, who was three and a half years old, and Kayla, who was only one and a half, required constant attention and care during the road trip. Nevertheless, I was determined to make the trip to see Tony graduate from boot camp, to celebrate his achievements, and to show him that we were proud of him. As I drove, I could not help but think about the sacrifices he had made to provide a better life for our family.

I hit a snag on the way there and ended up getting lost in Georgia, which was disheartening. However, I refused to let this setback deter me from my goal. Despite missing all of family day, I arrived in South Carolina that night, feeling anxious and exhausted. I booked a hotel room, knowing that the next day would be graduation day, and I needed to be well-rested to attend the ceremony.

The next morning, I woke up early, dressed in my best clothes, and headed to the graduation ceremony. My heart was pounding with excitement and anticipation as I walked through the crowds of families, all eager to see their loved one's graduate.

Finally, Tony marched onto the parade deck with his platoon, and I felt my heart swell with pride. He looked different, so skinny yet strong and confident in his uniform. He was standing tall and proud. As I looked at him, I could see how much he had changed. Seeing him walk across the parade deck filled my eyes with tears of joy and relief. I felt a sense of and respect and admiration for him.

After the ceremony, I rushed to hug Tony, feeling his embrace, and holding him close. It was a moment I would never forget, a moment that made all the hardships and struggles worth it. Seeing him graduate and knowing that he had accomplished his goal was a testament to his resilience and determination. It made me feel incredibly grateful and blessed to have him in my life.

Seeing Tony graduate from boot camp and becoming a Marine was a defining moment in our lives. It brought us closer together and gave us a newfound appreciation for the sacrifices we were making as a military family. As we drove back home with our girls, I felt a renewed sense of hope and determination to face whatever challenges lay ahead, knowing that we were stronger together.

After Tony's graduation, he was able to spend ten glorious days at home with our family. It was a much-needed break from the rigors of boot camp, and we savored every moment of his time with us. Tony was overjoyed to be home, and he immediately took charge of caring for our daughters. He played with Brianna and Kayla, taking them to the park and reading to them. Watching him bond with our children filled me with a sense of warmth and contentment.

Tony also made sure to pamper me during his visit home. He rubbed my growing belly and made sure I was always comfortable. It was wonderful to have him by my side again, and we spent every possible moment together. We took walks in the park, cooked meals together, and watched movies snuggled up on the couch. These ten days felt like a dream, a perfect bubble of happiness and love.

As Tony's visit ended, we both felt sad to say goodbye. However, we knew that he had a duty to fulfill, and we were proud to support him. We hugged each other tightly, promising to stay strong until we were together again. Those ten days were a reminder of why we were working so hard, why we were making so many sacrifices. Our love for each other and our family was worth it.

After Tony left for MCT school, the days felt long and lonely. I missed him terribly, but I knew that this was all part of the process. Tony was working hard to provide a better future for our family, and I was doing my best to hold things down at home. Despite the distance, we made it a point to talk every chance we got, and our conversations were filled with plans for our future. We talked about getting married soon, but we both knew that we did not have the money for a big wedding. However, we were determined to make it happen no matter what. In the meantime, I kept busy with our girls. As Tony completed his MOS training at Camp Lejeune, NC, I eagerly counted down the days until we could be reunited. When he finally returned home, I was overjoyed to have him back in my arms even for a little bit. We both knew that we wanted to spend the rest of our lives together, and we did not need a big ceremony or a lot of money to make that happen. All we needed was each other's love and commitment to make our dreams a reality.

Married at Twenty-One

Tony returned home on ten days of leave, and as soon as we were reunited, we knew we wanted to spend the rest of our lives together. We decided to take the leap and get married while he was back home. We have been talking about our marriage plans for a while now. On September 18, 1998, we made the bold move to head to the courthouse to get married.

Tony looked dashing in his sharp military uniform, and I chose a lovely baby blue dress that hugged my growing belly. I was nervous and excited at the same time. This was it. We were finally going to make it official.

As we arrived at the courthouse, our excitement was quickly dampened by the realization that we needed a marriage license first. Despite our youthful ignorance, we were undeterred. We knew that nothing was going to stop us from getting married. So, we planned to return the next day and get the necessary license.

As fate would have it, our setback at the courthouse led us to a serendipitous turn of events. Tony's mother suggested that he call his uncle, a pastor at a nearby church, and ask him to marry us. It seemed like a long shot, but Tony decided to do it. So, we headed off to obtain our marriage license and then made our way to the church to ask his uncle for his help.

To our delight and surprise, his uncle agreed to marry us! After talking to us for fifteen minutes his uncle married us in his small church, on September 19, 1998. It was an intimate and beautiful ceremony, with only my little sister and Tony's mom present.

As I exchanged vows with my beloved husband, I felt overwhelmed with happiness and joy. Tony's mom and my little sister looked on, their faces beaming with pride and love. It was a moment that we would always cherish, a symbol of our commitment to each other and the beginning of our journey as husband and wife.

After the ceremony, we decided to make a surprise visit to my aunt and uncle's house. My uncle was battling cancer and was under hospice care at home. Despite the joyous occasion, I was feeling a mix of emotions, including sadness and worry about my uncle's health. He had always been there for me, even when I was a child, and it was difficult to see him in such a vulnerable state.

When we arrived at their house, my uncle's face lit up with excitement. He was thrilled to see us all dressed up and ready to start our new life together. He complimented us on our appearance, saying how beautiful we looked, and told me how proud he was of me. His kind words and warm embrace were a reminder of how much he loved and cared for us.

After we left my aunt and uncle's house, we went out to lunch to celebrate our marriage and enjoyed the rest of the day together. Later that evening, we returned home to begin our journey as newlyweds. With my older sister watching the kids, Tony and I spent our first night together as a married couple at home. We spent hours reminiscing about how far we have come, talking about our hopes and dreams for the future, and basking in the warmth of our newfound love. It was a perfect start to our new life together, and we knew that we were embarking on a journey that would be full of love, adventure, and endless possibilities.

Just twelve days after our beautiful wedding, tragedy struck our family. My uncle, who had been battling cancer, passed away at the age of forty. He was a person who had left a lasting impression on everyone he met. He was kind, helpful, fun, caring, and loving. He lived life to the fullest and was always there for me when I needed him.

I was absolutely devastated by the news of his passing. It was hard to believe that he was no longer with us. I was also sad that he would never get to meet our new baby girl. During this difficult time, Tony was my rock. He was there for me every step of the way, supporting me and showing me unconditional love.

Tony was able to extend his leave and attend the funeral with me, which meant the world to me. His presence gave me strength, and I was so grateful to have him by my side during such a challenging time. We mourned my uncle's passing together and promised to keep his memory alive in our hearts. Despite the sadness, we were determined to focus on the positive moments in our lives and cherish every moment we had together.

Iwakuni Japan: September 1998-October 1999

Just when we thought we could not handle any more, life threw us yet another curveball. In the midst of our grief, Tony received the crushing news that he would be sent to Iwakuni, Japan, without our family for an entire year. It felt like a cruel joke. How could the military separate our family for such a long time? It did not seem fair.

I was completely blindsided by the news, and I could not stop crying. The thought of being apart from Tony for an entire year was unbearable. We had already been through so much together, and now we were facing yet another challenge. To make matters worse, I was seven months pregnant with our third daughter. He has been gone most of my pregnancy and I've been doing everything alone. How was I supposed to give birth without my husband by my side? How could I raise three children all alone?

The thought of Tony being so far away, unable to share in the precious moments of our daughter's birth and early childhood, was devastating. I felt lost and overwhelmed, unsure of how I would cope without him. It was a dark time in our lives, but somehow, we knew we had to find a way to get through it. We had each other, and that was the one thing that would never change.

As we prepared for Tony's departure, he wiped away my tears, Tony wrapped me in his arms and whispered, "I love you." His words filled me with comfort and hope. We promised to stay connected as much as possible, to share our experiences and support each other through every challenge. Tony reassured me that even though he was thousands of miles away, he would be with me every step of the way. So, three weeks after our marriage I watched Tony get on a plane and go across the world and fulfill his commitment. The love of my life, my newlywed husband, was leaving me for an entire year, my heart was shattered. I loved Tony more than anything, and I would do whatever it took to support him. I looked up at the sky, I whispered a silent prayer, asking for strength and guidance and to keep Tony safe and sound.

The weeks that followed were filled with anxiety and loneliness. Being separated from Tony was more challenging than I ever thought possible. Juggling work, caring for two energetic toddlers, and being pregnant was overwhelming. Trying to maintain a positive attitude and keep my spirits up was a daunting task. My days were long and exhausting, and the nights were even harder, with only the emptiness of our bed to keep me company. Tony's calls were like lifelines, keeping me connected to him and reminding me of his unwavering love. In those moments, his voice was the only thing keeping me from falling apart.

Despite the struggles, I could not help but feel a pang of jealousy for the new life Tony was experiencing in Japan. He was making new friends, trying new foods, exploring the beautiful city of Iwakuni, and participating in exciting military exercises. He was having the time of his life and experiencing all these new things without me.

Meanwhile, I was stuck at home in the projects, juggling work and the kids while feeling the weight of the pregnancy. It was very challenging, but I knew I had to be strong. Our life together was temporarily on hold, I knew that Tony's commitment to our family and his military service would only make us stronger. So, I remained steadfast in my faith that we would overcome this challenge together.

Courtney Ann: December 18, 1998

As I walked into my doctor's appointment, I felt a mixture of excitement and anxiety. With my due date fast approaching and Tony still thousands of miles away in Japan, I was nervous about the birth of our third child. My doctor's calm and reassuring demeanor put me at ease. He explained that he wanted to schedule an induction, just in case I went into labor on Christmas Day.

I spent the next few days preparing for the birth, making arrangements for my older sister to watch our two daughters and my little sister to assist me during delivery. Having my family's support was a great comfort to me, especially with Tony being so far away.

As Christmas approached, I went into the hospital and got induced. Despite the hustle and bustle of the holiday season, the labor went smoothly. In just a few pushes, I welcomed our third daughter, Courtney Ann, into the world. Her head was full of hair, and she had the most beautiful brown eyes I had ever seen. The joy I felt in that moment was indescribable. I could not believe I was now a mother of three wonderful girls, just like my own mom. It was a truly magical time, and I was grateful for the love and support of my family.

As soon as our little girl was born, I felt a rush of emotions that I could not wait to share with Tony. Through a Red Cross message, I shared the most wonderful news - that we had welcomed a healthy and beautiful daughter into the world. After the message, I waited eagerly for his call. Then finally the phone rang a few hours later. I described every detail to him - the way she looked, the sound of her cry, and how her tiny hand wrapped around my finger. As I spoke, tears streamed down my face, and I knew that Tony could feel the love and joy emanating from my voice. Even though he could not be there in person to hold our precious baby, his words were filled with pride and affection, and I felt his love across the miles. It was a moment that I would always cherish, and a testament to the power of love and family, even in the face of distance and adversity.

Challenges Ahead

Life in the projects of Covington, KY, was far from easy, but it was filled with a love so strong it could overcome any obstacle. As a mother of three little girls, every day was a new challenge, but it was also an opportunity to create precious memories with my family. Despite having a stable job at a law firm, I made the bold decision to quit and become a stay-at-home mom. The cost of daycare for three children was simply too steep, and I knew that being there for my daughters was the best choice for our family.

As I settled into my new role as a full-time caregiver, I faced many obstacles, including loneliness and boredom. However, my little sister became a bright ray of sunshine in my life. She was always there to lend a helping hand and provide a much-needed dose of laughter when things got tough. Her unwavering support gave me the strength to keep going, even on the darkest days.

Through the ups and downs of motherhood, I found inspiration in the unconditional love my children gave me. Their joy and laughter filled my heart with warmth and gratitude. I also found solace in the knowledge that I was doing everything in my power to give them the best possible life.

As I reflect on those challenging but rewarding days, I cannot help but wonder what other twists and turns life has in store for me. But one thing is for sure: no matter what happens, I will always cherish the memories of raising my three precious little girls in a place that taught us the true meaning of love, resilience, and hope.

The memories of a once-cherished love started to blur as the days passed without a call or a letter from Tony. I felt an unshakable worry, a fear that something had gone terribly wrong. Then that fateful day came, the day I received a letter that crushed my heart. In it, Tony told me that he did not want to be with me anymore. How could this be? We were married; we had built a life together. The weight of confusion and pain bore down on me, and I felt lost, completely alone.

Desperate for help, I went Tony's mother house, and we contacted the Red Cross, hoping to get a message to him. To them, it was not an emergency, and days passed by in a blur of mounting desperation. Then, finally, a call came through. It was Tony on the other end of the line, and my heart filled with hope. His words sliced through me like a sharp blade - he liked his freedom overseas, and he wanted to do his own thing. I was stunned, utterly heartbroken. All the love we had shared, the memories we had made, were they all for nothing.

The weight of his betrayal felt like a crushing wave, and I struggled to pick up the shattered pieces of my life. It was a dizzying, emotional time. Even as I was drowning in a sea of emotions, I found the strength and resilience within myself to keep moving forward. I knew that I had to pick up the pieces and rebuild my life, no matter how hard it may be.

The future loomed before me like a dark abyss, and the weight of being a single parent to three young children was almost too much to bear. The thought of supporting us on my own was terrifying, and fear and uncertainty filled my heart. I knew that I had to stay strong for my kids, to be there for them no matter what. I resolved to put on a brave face and soldier on, even when it felt like everything was falling apart.

Though my heart still ached from the pain and heartbreak of our failed marriage, Tony would occasionally check in on us. It was a small comfort to know that he still cared about our children, even if he no longer wanted to be with me. Still, every day felt like a new challenge, and I struggled to keep my head above water. Even in the midst of it all, I found inspiration in the smiles and laughter of my little ones. They were my light in the darkness, my reason for pushing forward.

Every step was a challenge, but I refused to give up. Even when the days felt endless and the nights seemed to stretch on forever, I kept going, kept searching for a glimmer of hope in the darkness. With each passing day, I grew stronger, more determined to overcome the obstacles in my path. As I watched my children grow and thrive, I knew that everything was worth it. Together, we would find a way forward, no matter what life throws our way.

The morning Tony called me; I knew something was wrong. His voice was strained, and there was an edge of fear that I had never heard before. My heart sank as he delivered the news that would possibly change our lives forever: he had been arrested, suspected of selling drugs and being involved in a gang with other Marines.

My mind raced as I struggled to comprehend what he was saying. Tony insisted that he was innocent, but he also knew of some Marines in his unit who were guilty. I did not know what to think. He did sell drugs before he went into the military. He confessed to drinking heavily and hanging out with the wrong crowd, and his desperation was palpable as he begged for another chance with me and our family.

Against my better judgement, I allowed myself to believe in his promises and forgave him. It was a difficult decision, but I loved him, and I wanted to believe that he was telling the truth. As it turned out, Tony was found not guilty, but he did receive a page eleven write-up.

A few months later, Tony would be returning home and off to a new duty station. Despite the drama and turmoil of that time, I could not help but feel a little bit of hope for our future together. This was a wake-up call for Tony, a chance for him to turn his life around and make amends for his mistakes.

I knew that our journey would not be easy, and that there were still many challenges ahead. In that moment, I felt a flicker of hope for our future together. Maybe this was the turning point we needed, a chance to build a stronger, more resilient love that could withstand anything that life throws our way. Who knows, our love story would have a happy ending after all, filled with romance, inspiration, and the knowledge that we had overcome the toughest of obstacles together.

Camp Lejeune, NC: October 1999-July 2004

I remember the day when Tony finally returned home from Japan. It was such a long-awaited moment that my heart was racing with anticipation. I could not wait for him to finally meet our ten-month-old daughter Courtney. Despite her shyness, she warmed up to him quickly. Brianna and Kayla were overjoyed to have their daddy home. The feeling of completeness and happiness was palpable in the air as we hugged and laughed together. It was a moment that I would always cherish in my heart. After spending so much time apart, it felt like we were finally a family again, and it was time to start our new adventure together.

As excited as I was for Tony's new orders, I could not help feeling a sense of trepidation. Leaving behind everything we knew in Cincinnati was both exhilarating and terrifying. I could not wait to leave the projects in Covington, KY. The thought of starting a new life in a new place was exciting and scary.

Saying goodbye to our family and friends was bittersweet. We had grown up with them, shared countless memories, and now it was time to leave them behind. We knew that this was an opportunity for a fresh start, a chance to explore the unknown and embark on a new adventure.

With the help of movers, we packed up our belongings and began the long ten-hour drive to Camp Lejeune, NC. As we drove, I could not help but feel a mix of emotions - excitement, fear, and hope. I knew that the journey ahead was going to be challenging, but I was ready to face it head-on.

Finally arriving in North Carolina was both exhilarating and overwhelming. We were starting from nothing, but it was a chance to create a new life for ourselves. Despite the challenges and uncertainties that lay ahead, I felt a sense of hope for our family's future. We were finally living the dream I had always envisioned - a happy, complete family with a world of possibilities before us.

Our family was thrusted into a whole new world as military members. Despite my father's previous service in the Airforce when I was younger, I found myself completely unprepared for the lifestyle as an adult. The military language and customs were foreign to me, and I realized there was a lot to learn. Our first obstacle was housing, as the waitlist for on-base accommodations was over a year long. We rented a double-wide trailer off base and began the process of adjusting to our new environment.

As a stay-at-home mom and wife, I struggled to find my footing in this unfamiliar place. With three young children to care for and only one car between us, the challenges were dreadful. I used to drive Tony to and from work so I could have a car during the day. The meager budget of only one-thousand dollars a month added another layer of stress to our already tight situation. I also became home sick. I missed my family and friends. Tony, my husband, was also in the process of adjusting after being stationed in Japan for a year. He was used to doing whatever he wanted and not having to worry about taking care of kids. Despite these difficulties, we were determined to make the most of our situation.

As we slowly acclimated to military life, I discovered a newfound respect for the sacrifices that military families make. The long hours, frequent moves, and uncertainty of deployments were challenges that we had to learn to navigate together. Through it all, we became a tight knit family that relied on each other for support. Looking back, I am proud of the strength and determination that we showed during that period of our lives. We were twenty-two years old with three kids trying to find our way in the world. Our journey was not easy, but it was an experience that brought us closer together and made us appreciate the sacrifices that military families make for their country.

Pregnancy #4

The news of our fourth pregnancy was a mix of emotions - excitement, joy, and a healthy dose of anxiety. Our family was already struggling financially, and the thought of adding another member to our already stretched resources was frightening. Tony was hoping for a son to continue the family name, but our doctor revealed that we were expecting another girl. Though we were thrilled to welcome a new member to our family, there was also a twinge of disappointment at the realization that we would not be having a son.

Despite the mixed emotions, the pregnancy became a turning point in our relationship. We spent hours talking about our hopes and dreams for our growing family, and together we tried to figure out how we could provide for everyone on our limited budget. I was happy that he would be there for me during this pregnancy. The shared experience of expecting a child, coupled with the challenges we faced, strengthened our bond, at least for a little while.

As my pregnancy progressed, I found myself feeling increasingly isolated and alone in my new military life. I had hoped that the impending arrival of our fourth child would bring Tony and me closer together, but instead, he continued to spend most of his free time with his military friends. Left alone to take care of our three young girls, I felt overwhelmed and unsupported.

Despite our best efforts, we were struggling to navigate the challenges of being a military family in a new place with limited support and resources. As the due date approached, our discussions turned to the possibility of separating after the baby was born. The strain on our relationship was real, and we both felt like we were drowning in the challenges of our new life.

Despite feeling alone in my new military life, I remained strong for our children and looked forward to welcoming our new baby girl into the family. I spent countless hours preparing for her arrival, making sure that everything was in order and that her siblings were excited about her impending arrival. As the due date approached, we were all filled with a sense of anticipation and joy.

At the same time, we knew that this would be our last child. I had decided to get my tubes tied, a difficult but necessary decision for us given our financial struggles and the challenges of military life. It was a bittersweet time for us, as we looked forward to the arrival of our new baby girl while also saying goodbye to the possibility of having any more children.

Surprise! Anthony Javone Jr: August 10, 2000

Tony and I had always had a tumultuous relationship but being a military family had added a whole new layer of complexity to our lives. With the due date for our fourth and last daughter fast approaching, we found ourselves struggling to navigate the challenges of being away from our hometown and the support of our family and friends.

As the day of the birth drew closer, our relationship continued to be a rollercoaster of emotions. We were both excited and anxious about the arrival of our new baby girl, but at the same time, we were also struggling to connect with each other.

When the time came for me to be induced, we were all together in the hospital room - Tony, the kids, and me. Then the nurses informed us that the kids would not be allowed in the room during the delivery. With no one else to watch them, Tony and I were faced with a difficult decision. In the end, we made the painful choice for Tony to take the kids home while I gave birth alone.

It was a tough decision, but we knew it was the best one for our family. I did not have time to be sad. I was determined to do whatever it took to bring our baby safely into the world, even if that meant facing the delivery alone.

As I went into labor, I could feel the baby coming quickly, and I knew that I did not have much time. I had hoped to get an epidural, but before I knew it, the pain was almost unbearable, and the baby was ready to be born.

The nurses urged me to wait, telling me that the doctor would be there soon, but I could feel my strength growing. Suddenly, I found myself pushing with all my might, and after just three pushes, I felt a wave of relief wash over me. I looked up, expecting to see the doctor, but instead, I saw a whole team of nurses in the room.

Then, the nurses shouted, "it's a boy." I looked in confusion and my heart leapt with joy. They placed my almost nine-pound baby boy on my chest, and I could not help but cry tears of happiness. Even though I had given birth alone, the moment was filled with pure joy and elation. I could not believe it - after three beautiful daughters, I had finally been given the best surprise of all: a healthy and beautiful baby boy.

As I held my newborn son in my arms, tears streamed down my face as I thought about the emotional rollercoaster that had led me to this moment. Giving birth alone was a heart-wrenching experience, but the joy of hearing the nurses shout "it's a boy" made it all worth it. I could not wait to share the news with Tony and the kids.

When I finally called, Tony's voice crackled with emotion as he struggled to believe the news. He started shouting with excitement. We both were in shock that we were blessed with a baby boy. The girls were so excited to have a baby brother. Things had been rocky, but in that moment, our shared joy brought us closer together. The miracle of our baby boy left us both feeling awash with newfound love.

After the birth of our unexpected baby boy, Tony rushed to the store to buy clothes and other necessities for him. As we had three daughters, we had nothing for a boy. The realization that we had a son was surreal, and we were both still in shock. I felt relieved that I had gone through with the procedure to get my tubes tied, but a part of me felt sad that I would never experience the miracle of childbirth again. However, the overwhelming love I felt for my new baby boy overshadowed any other emotions. We spent the next few days bonding with our son, and I could not help but feel grateful for this unexpected blessing.

Despite the challenges we had faced as a military family, the arrival of our son brought us closer together and filled our hearts with joy. Our little boy was the light of our life, and he brought us closer than we ever thought possible. He reminded us of the love that we shared, and the strength that we had as a family. It was a tough journey, but in the end, it was all worth it. As we looked at our beautiful family of six, we knew that we were blessed beyond measure, and we were excited for all that the future held for us.

Difficult Times at Camp Lejeune, NC

As a twenty-three-year-old mother of four, life was a whirlwind for me and Tony. Our children's ages ranged from five to newborn, and adjusting to our new life as a military family was demanding. I often felt overwhelmed and isolated, but Tony's excitement at the prospect of raising a son brought us closer together. Our relationship was flourishing, and we were grateful for every moment we spent as a family.

After months and months of waiting, we finally received the call we had been waiting for, and we moved into base housing. It was a big four-bedroom house with a yard. I was eager to get moved in and make it a home. Also, it was a relief to be surrounded by other military families, but we still faced unique challenges. Our oldest daughter Brianna was in kindergarten, and our second daughter Kayla was in preschool for half the day, which gave me a brief break during the day.

Unfortunately, our newfound stability was short-lived, and our relationship was being tested once again. It was always something. It felt like the universe was against us. Just as we thought things were looking up, life would throw us another curveball. We tried to keep our heads up and push through, but it felt like nothing stayed good for too long. The stress of being a military family, adjusting to new environments, and dealing with the difficulties of life was taking its toll on us. It was a constant battle to keep our relationship strong and maintain a sense of normalcy for our children.

As a military family, we were no strangers to challenges. We had already been through so much. Just when we thought we had overcome it all, life decided to throw us another plot twist. Tony's field exercises left me feeling more isolated and alone than ever before. With him gone, I had to take care of everything - the kids, the house, and all day-to-day responsibilities. It was exhausting, but I knew I had to be strong for the sake of our family.

Then, one night, I received a call that no military spouse ever wants to get - Tony had been injured. A forklift had run over his foot in the field, and the extent of his injuries was still unknown. I was panicked, waiting for any news about his condition. I packed up all the kids in the middle of the night and rushed over to the hospital. I did not know what to accept.

After what felt like an eternity, I finally got to see Tony. He was in a lot of pain but thankfully he had only suffered a bad ankle sprain. It was such a relief to know that he was going to be okay. His unit did not give him any time to rest because he had to be back at work the next day. He had to prepare for another field exercise in a month. I was terrified at the thought of being alone again.

The day before Tony was set to leave for the field again it was like any other day. I was busy cleaning up around the house and trying to spend some quality time with Tony before his departure. As I was walking through the garage, I slipped and fell. The pain was excruciating, and I knew immediately that something was seriously wrong. Tony quickly got the kids into the car and rushed me to the hospital.

At the hospital, I found out that I had broken my ankle and needed surgery to fix it. The thought of surgery terrified me, but I knew I had no other choice. I had the surgery a few days later, where the doctors put a plate and screws into my ankle. Recovery was not easy, and Tony's absence during the initial stages made it even harder. Two days after my surgery Tony had to continue with his field exercise for a month. I was left to care for our four young children, including our 9-month-old baby, while dealing with the pain and discomfort of my injury.

Looking back at that time in my life, it is hard to believe how I managed to do it all. After breaking my ankle and undergoing surgery, I was left to take care of our four children all on my own. I could not rely on Tony to help me with the kids or with household chores, as he was still away on field duty. It was an impossible challenge, but I was determined to be strong for my family.

I remember having to rely on crutches to get around, and driving was no easy task. Simple tasks like climbing stairs to take a bath or cooking dinner for the kids was extremely difficult. I refused to let my injury and Tony's absence break me.

I had to take charge of everything and keep our household running smoothly. I had to manage the kids' schedules, cook, clean, and do laundry. It was an exhausting time, but I remained focused on being strong and resilient.

Eventually, I started to regain my strength and some mobility, which was a huge relief. I knew that I had come out of that challenging time even stronger than before. I learned the importance of being independent, resourceful, and persevering through adversity. It was a valuable lesson that has stayed with me to this day.

With Tony finally home from the field, I was able to breathe a little easier. His help with the kids and the household chores were invaluable as I continued to recover from my broken ankle. However, something seemed off with him. He was withdrawn and quiet, not like his usual self. At first, I thought it was just exhaustion from his time in the field, but the days turned into weeks, and I could not ignore it anymore. I started to worry that something serious was going on with him, but he refused to talk about it. I tried everything to get him to open up - from gentle coaxing to more direct approaches - but nothing seemed to work. It felt like we were drifting apart.

As the strain on our marriage grew, I found myself wondering where we went wrong. Tony's nights out with his friends became more frequent and longer, leaving me to take care of our four children alone. I felt like a single parent, exhausted, and overwhelmed by the responsibility.

I tried talking to Tony, explaining how I felt neglected and unimportant. Our conversations always ended in arguments. He did not seem to understand why I was so upset and accused me of overreacting. I began to question if he even cared about our family and his responsibilities as a husband and father.

Despite my attempts to hold our marriage together, I could not shake the feeling that we were headed for a divorce. I felt trapped and alone, wondering if I would ever find happiness again. It was a difficult time in my life, but I knew that I needed to do what was best for myself and my children.

In January 2001, our family faced a heartbreaking tragedy. Tony's father passed away suddenly, and just hours later, his uncle also died of a heart attack upon hearing the news. Tony was not close to his father, and he had not spoken to him in a while, but he was still hurt and sad. I never got to meet his father. Tony had to travel back to Cincinnati alone to attend the funerals, leaving us behind. It was a tough time for all of us. We could not go with Tony because we did not have the extra money because we just returned home from Cincinnati during Christmas time.

We missed Tony and worried about him, while also grieving for the loss of his loved ones. When Tony returned home, he seemed different. His normally outgoing personality was replaced by a quiet and withdrawn demeanor. I tried to support him as best I could, but it seemed like nothing I did or said could bring him out of his funk.

As days turned into weeks, my suspicions about Tony's behavior continued to grow. He was distant and secretive, and I could not shake the feeling that something was wrong. It was like he was living in his own world, and I was not a part of it anymore. I decided to confront him, but he brushed me off and said he was just tired from work and stressed about our finances. I tried to believe him, but my gut told me otherwise.

One day, when he was at work, I decided to do some snooping around the house. I checked our phone bill and found numbers I did not recognize. Then, I stumbled upon something that shattered my world. In Tony's military trunk, I found recent letters from his ex-girlfriend. They were love letters, written after his father's funeral, talking about how they had been together. I felt sick to my stomach. All this time, I had been trusting him, but he had been lying to me. I was devastated and wondered if he had cheated on me with other women. My trust in him was broken, and I did not know if we could ever recover from this. I did not know what to do. Should I confront him? I decided to confront him right away. When he got home, I asked him if he was cheating on me, and at first, he denied anything was going on. But then, I showed him the evidence, and he broke down and confessed. He told me that after his father's funeral he went to see his ex-girlfriend and they took things too far.

The next few weeks were a blur of tears and heartache. We tried to talk things out, but it seemed like every conversation ended in an argument. I felt betrayed and hurt, and I could not believe that the man I had trusted for so long had been lying to me. I wondered how many other women he had been with and how long the affair had been going on.

The trust had been completely broken, and I found myself constantly questioning his every move. I could not escape the feeling of being inadequate and unworthy of love, no matter how hard I tried to shake it off. I felt like my world was crumbling down. The man I loved, trusted, and built a family with had shattered my heart into a million pieces. I could not eat, sleep, or even function properly. I wanted to die. I wanted all the pain to go away. I was completely blindsided and shattered. It was like a never-ending nightmare that I could not escape from, as I hit rock bottom.

As I struggled to come to terms with Tony's betrayal, I found myself facing a deep inner turmoil that threatened to consume me. I was going through Tony's things and phone records constantly. The once enthusiastic love I had for Tony was now replaced with a mixture of anger, hurt, and disappointment. I was constantly haunted by thoughts of his infidelity, wondering if he was still seeing other women behind my back.

As I delved deeper into Tony's betrayal, the pain and hurt I felt grew exponentially. The constant nagging feeling of being not enough and inadequate was a heavy burden to bear. I felt like I was living in a perpetual state of agony, where the pain and hurt were so intense that it felt like a physical wound that would never heal.

The days seemed endless, and I found myself constantly obsessing over every little detail of Tony's actions, searching for any sign of deception. I felt like I was going crazy, as the trust we once had had been shattered, leaving a void in its place.

The world around me had lost its colors, and I found myself struggling to find the strength to carry on. The once happy memories I had with Tony were now tainted, and I could not escape the feeling of betrayal and hurt.

I became so consumed with self-blame that I was convinced that I was the reason for Tony's infidelity. It was as if I had failed in every aspect of our relationship. The weight of my thoughts was suffocating, and I could not escape the feeling that I was drowning in a sea of sadness and pain.

The days turned into weeks, and the weeks turned into months, but the pain remained. I wondered if I would ever be able to trust anyone again, or if the scars of Tony's infidelity would remain with me forever. It was a dark time in our relationship, and I did not know if we could ever come back from it.

The tension in the air was thick as we tried to navigate our way back to a healthy relationship. It seemed like no matter what we did, the arguments kept coming. Every disagreement felt like a personal attack, and we both found ourselves feeling hurt and defensive. It was like walking on a tightrope, with one wrong move potentially leading to a disastrous fall. I tried to stay positive and keep the faith, but it was difficult to ignore the fear and uncertainty that gnawed at my insides. Our once passionate love had become a warzone. It was as if we were in a never-ending cycle of love, betrayal, and heartbreak, and I did not know how much longer I could take it.

As I tried to navigate my feelings, I began to realize that sometimes love is not enough to keep a relationship together. Trust, honesty, and open communication were just as crucial as love in a successful marriage. Tony's betrayal had broken the foundation of our relationship, and I did not know if it could ever be rebuilt. I was torn between wanting to save our marriage and the fear of being hurt again. The path forward was murky and uncertain, but I knew that I needed time to think and figure out what was best for me and my family.

As I tried to heal from the pain, Tony started to be very apologetic and sweet towards me. Tony's tearful apology was a ray of hope in my otherwise dark and gloomy life. The prospect of saving our marriage was tempting, but I could not shake off the feeling that something was still wrong. I wanted to believe him, but I could not stop the nagging feeling in my gut that this would not be the last time he betrayed me. Even though he said he was sorry and that it was over, I felt like I could not trust him anymore. His betrayal had shattered my faith in him and our marriage, leaving me feeling lost and confused.

As Tony continued to do and say all the right things, I started to feel myself coming out of my funk and slowly trusting him again. Our determination to make our marriage work was palpable and gave us both hope. Our love was rekindling. I was feeling hopeful, and I loved Tony with all my heart and soul.

Then small arguments quickly escalated into heated exchanges, and soon we found ourselves walking on eggshells around each other. I did not know how to fix things, and I was terrified that our love story was about to come to an abrupt and tragic end.

Breaking Point

The moment I found out Tony was talking to another ex, my heart plummeted to my stomach. He had promised that their relationship was over. When I confronted him, he brushed it off as a harmless conversation and insisted that she was "just a friend." I knew better than to believe him.

As the days went on, my suspicions grew stronger. Tony would sneak away and talk on the phone. When I asked him about it, he became defensive and said it was not any of my business who he was talking to. It was clear that he was hiding something.

The days after I kicked Tony out of the house were some of the loneliest of my life. We spent months apart, with him only coming over once a week to see the kids. I was not sure what I was going to do without him, but I knew that I could not keep living in a relationship where I could not trust him.

However, as time went on, I started to think that maybe things were headed in the right direction. Tony seemed genuinely remorseful, and he promised that he was committed to making things work between us. Despite my reservations, I decided to give him another chance.

But as the saying goes, old habits die hard. One night, Tony stayed over, and I could not help but feel uneasy. I still did not fully trust him, so I went through his wallet.

That is when I found it: an ATM receipt from Cincinnati, Ohio. My heart sank as I realized that he had gone back home without telling me. A long weekend had just passed, and I knew that he had spent it with his ex.

I confronted him about it, and at first, he tried to deny it. When I pulled out the receipt, he could not lie anymore. He finally confessed to being in Cincinnati over the weekend, and I was livid. How could he betray me again after everything we had been through?

I was left feeling devastated and heartbroken. As the days went on, I realized that I deserved better than someone who could not be honest and faithful. I knew that it was time to end things for good. The thought of living without him was scary, but it was better than being with someone who could not be faithful to me. I was ready to move on and find someone who would treat me with the love and respect I deserved.

Despite my reservations, I gave Tony another chance. He pleaded with me, crying, and promising that he would stop talking to his ex. He wanted to be a family, and he was willing to do anything to make me stay. I was so in love with him, and I was scared to start over with four young kids and no job, so I took him back.

At first, everything was great. We worked hard to repair our relationship, but it did not take long for us to slip back into our old patterns. We were fighting and arguing constantly, and I found myself unable to trust him. I began going through his things and checking our phone records for any signs of infidelity.

One day, I discovered that he was still talking to his ex, despite promising to cut all ties with her. I was heartbroken, and I confronted him about it. He got defensive and told me that they were just friends and that I needed to get over it. I could not believe what I was hearing. I gave him an ultimatum: stop talking to her, or I would pack up the kids and leave.

But he refused. He told me that he was not going to stop talking to her, that he wanted her in his life. In that moment, I knew that I had to leave. He was choosing her over me and our family, and I could not stay in a relationship where I was second best. It was one of the hardest decisions I have ever made, but I knew it was the right one.

Leaving Tony behind was one of the toughest decisions of my life, but deep down, I knew it was the right thing to do. As I packed up our belongings, I could not help but feel a sense of sadness wash over me. This was not the life I had imagined for myself and my children.

As we said our goodbyes, tears streamed down all our faces, and my heart felt like it was breaking into a billion pieces. Tony, too, was crying, and it was clear that he was remorseful for his actions. As much as I wanted to forgive him, I knew that I could not continue living with someone who had betrayed my trust.

As we drove away, I felt a mix of emotions: sadness, regret, uncertainty, and fear. The road ahead was long and winding, and I knew that it would not be an easy journey. I was determined to keep moving forward and find a love that was true and unwavering, even if it meant starting over from scratch.

The first few hours of the drive were the toughest. My children were sobbing in the backseat, and I could feel my own tears welling up. I was exhausted from the packing and the emotional turmoil, but I knew that I could not stop. I needed to get away as quickly as possible, and Cincinnati felt like the safest place to go.

Despite the exhaustion and the emotional turmoil, I kept driving. My mind was racing with all kinds of thoughts and questions: What would happen next? Would we find a new home and a new life? Would I be able to provide for my children on my own? In the midst of it all, there was one thing that I was sure of: I deserved better than what Tony had to offer, and I was determined to find it.

The few days I spent in Cincinnati were emotionally draining, and I knew I could not stay there for long. So, I made my way to Kansas City, MO, where my mom and little sister were living at the time. Starting from scratch was overwhelming, especially as a young woman with four children to care for. I was determined to create a better life for us and not let Tony's betrayal define me.

Despite the challenges I faced, I refused to lose hope and held onto the belief that things would get better. Life in Kansas City was not going to be easy, but with the help of my mom and little sister, I started looking for a job and enrolled my daughter Brianna back in school. It was a scary task to start over, but I began to feel like things were going to be okay.

As the days went by, I grew more confident in my ability to make a better life for myself and my children. It was not easy, and the road ahead was full of obstacles, but I was ready to face them with grit and determination. My journey is a reminder that even in the face of adversity, we have the power to rise above it all and create a better future for ourselves.

About two weeks after I left, Tony called me, and I was taken aback by the quivering tone of his voice. He begged me to come back home, telling me how much he missed us and the kids. He made a solemn vow never to talk to his ex-again and promised to do everything in his power to make our marriage work. He even proposed going to counseling and wanting to attend church.

At first, I stood my ground and refused his pleas, knowing how much his words had hurt me. As the days passed, his constant phone calls, day, and night, started wearing me down, and eventually, I caved in. Everything in me was pulling me back to him. I believed in second chances, and I hoped that Tony had changed.

A month later, I packed up the kids and drove back to Camp Lejeune, giving our marriage another chance. Despite everything that had happened, I still loved Tony and was hopeful that we could find our way back to each other. I was determined to try one last time for the sake of our children.

However, things were not as easy as I had hoped. Tony's promises were short-lived, and it did not take long for his old ways to resurface. It was a constant battle, and I found myself struggling to keep my head above water. We both tried to make our marriage work, but old habits die hard, and we kept falling back into the same patterns. Our fights were explosive, and I could not help but bring up the past and the pain he had caused me. We were both lost, young, and without any guidance, and it seemed like we were barely hanging on.

As time went on, I began to realize that I deserved better than a life filled with constant turmoil and emotional pain. I wanted a life where I felt safe, loved, and respected. I knew deep down that leaving Tony was the right decision, but the thought of starting over was daunting. I did not want to uproot the kids again, so I stayed and tried to come up with a plan to start over when the time was right.

September 11, 2001

On that fateful September day in 2001, history was forever changed. The world watched in horror as terrorists hijacked four planes, resulting in unimaginable destruction and loss of life. Two planes crashed into the Twin Towers of the World Trade Center in New York City, causing them to collapse. Another plane hit the Pentagon in Washington, D.C., while the fourth plane crashed in a field in Pennsylvania.

At the time, I had no idea that my life was about to be forever altered by these events. I went to Anthony Jr's doctor appointment that morning, completely unaware of the tragedy that was unfolding. However, as I was walking around the PX on base, I saw the news playing on the screens, and I knew something terrible had happened. I rushed home and turned on the TV, unable to believe what I was seeing.

As I rushed to pick up my daughters from school, the air was thick with tension. The news had been flooded with reports of the horrific terrorist attacks that had shaken the country to its core. I could not shake off the feeling of unease that settled deep within me as I collected my girls. The chaos of the world had seeped into our military town, and I did not know what the future held for us.

Just as we reached our home on the military base, Tony's call came through. The base was on lockdown, and we were to stay put until further notice. Later that evening I had to pick up Tony from work. As I drove throughout base to get him, the sight of tanks and Marines armed with guns on every corner was almost too much to bear. It was like something out of a movie - surreal and terrifying all at once.

Our military IDs were checked at every turn, and we were not allowed to leave the base. The world outside was changing at an unprecedented pace, and we were powerless to stop it. As we huddled together in front of the TV, the images of the Twin Towers falling, and the Pentagon burning etched themselves into our minds. Fear and uncertainty became our constant companions, and we wondered if Tony would have to deploy. Our lives had been irrevocably changed, and we had no choice but to try and cope with the new reality that had been thrust upon us.

The attacks on September 11, 2001, not only changed the world but also took a toll on my relationship with Tony. Prior to the tragedy, we were already struggling, and in the aftermath, we grew more distant. It felt like we were trying to process the tragedy on our own, and our communication suffered as a result.

The drama of our relationship was heightened by the fear and uncertainty that gripped us all. The belief that our love would get us through anything, seemed to fade away. We were both struggling to cope with the enormity of what had happened, and it was taking a toll on us in ways we could not have predicted. As the weeks went by, we both were waiting to see if Tony would have to deploy, adding another layer of uncertainty to our already fragile relationship.

The events of 9/11 were a day of tragedy and terror, but they also showed me how fragile life can be. It made me realize that we never know what the future holds and that we should cherish every moment we have with our loved ones. The attacks brought people from all walks of life together in grief and unity, and it reminded us that even in the darkest moments, there is still hope.

In the aftermath of 9/11, life changed for many of us. Security measures were heightened, and fear and uncertainty became a part of daily life. Through it all, we learned to be strong and resilient, and we never forgot those who lost their lives that day. The events of 9/11 will forever be etched in my memory as a reminder of the fragility of life and the power of human resilience.

Deployment to Jordan: March 2002- September 2002

In March 2002, Tony received orders to deploy to Jordan to support Operation Enduring Freedom, and my heart sank as I watched him pack his bags and prepare to leave. I could not shake the fear and sadness that had taken hold of me, knowing that he would be gone for six long months. The idea of him being in a possible war zone made my stomach churn with worry, and I felt like I was losing my grip on reality.

As I watched him walk out the door, I knew that the next few months would be some of the toughest of our lives. Little did I know that this deployment would also become a turning point for our relationship.

Tony and I were still struggling in our relationship, and the thought of Tony being gone for such a long time made me wonder if we would even make it through this. With him gone, I would be left to take care of our four young children all alone. They were ages seven, five, three, and one, and the thought of being responsible for them without any help filled me with nervousness and trepidation.

Adding to my worries was the fact that I was many states away from my family and did not have many friends in the area. The thought of facing this challenge alone was overwhelming, and I found myself questioning whether I could do it. Should I leave and move back to Cincinnati, where I would have more support? Or should I stay put and not uproot the kids? The uncertainty of what to do next left me feeling lost and confused.

Tony and I had many discussions about what to do next, and we decided that I would stay in North Carolina with the kids until he returned from his deployment. We agreed that we would discuss our next steps together once he was back home safe.

Tony's deployment was a particularly tough test of our resilience. The thought of him in harm's way weighed heavily on my heart, but I drew strength from his bravery and dedication to his country. He was our hero, and we were proud of him.

The countdown to Tony's return was both exhilarating and nerve-wracking. I tried to keep my spirits up and stay positive, but there were moments when I could not help but worry about what might happen next.

As the days ticked by, I held onto hope and looked forward to the day when we would be reunited. The kids and I found ways to stay busy despite the distance. We also exchanged letters and emails with Tony and talked on the phone every now and then.

During Tony's deployment, he had a lot of time to reflect on his life and his priorities. Being in danger made him realize what was truly important to him. He wanted to make our marriage work and be a happy, loving family. He also recognized how much he had hurt me in the past and apologized for his mistakes.

Tony promised me that he would not talk to any of his exes anymore and that his past was all behind him now. His words were so romantic and heartfelt that they touched my heart, and I felt hopeful for our future together. We talked about our dreams for our family, and he pledged to do whatever it took to keep us together.

It was a turning point for us, a moment of clarity and commitment. Tony finally chose me, he chose us, our family. I knew then that we were in this together, no matter what.

The days, weeks, and months of Tony's deployment felt like an eternity. We got through it together, one day at a time. I was so proud of him for his bravery and dedication, and his strength inspired me to be strong for our family while he was away.

Then, finally, the day arrived when Tony returned home safely. It was an emotional and powerful moment, one that we had been waiting for and dreaming of for so long. As we hugged each other tightly and cried tears of joy, it felt like all the pain and uncertainty of the past months melted away.

The drama of Tony's homecoming was unforgettable. It was a moment of pure relief and happiness, a reminder of the power of love to overcome even the toughest of challenges. In that moment, we were reminded of what was tremendously important in life - family, love, and togetherness.

As we settled back into our daily routine, we were grateful for every moment that we spent together. We knew that we had been through something incredibly difficult and that we had come out stronger on the other side. We were reminded once again that no matter what life throws our way, we will always be in this together.

Deployment to Bahrain: December 2002-June 2003

Just when we thought that everything was finally falling back into place, life had another surprise in store for us. Tony received news that he would be deploying again, this time to Bahrain. It had only been three months since he had returned home from his last deployment, and the thought of him leaving again was devastating.

The news of Tony's upcoming deployment hit me like a ton of bricks. It felt like we had just gotten our family back together, and now he was being taken away from us once again. I could not believe that he would have to leave us so soon after coming home, and the thought of being alone with the kids was overwhelming.

Despite Tony's reassurances that everything would be okay, I could not shake the feeling of sadness and loss. It was hard to imagine our daily routines without him, and the thought of having to do it all over again was almost too much to bear.

As the days went by, we tried to make the most of the time we had left together. We went on family trips, took lots of pictures, and created memories that we could hold onto while he was gone. No matter how much we tried to distract ourselves, the looming thought of his departure was always present, casting a shadow over our moments of joy.

When the day finally came for him to leave, it was one of the hardest moments of my life. Tears streamed down my face as I hugged him tightly, not wanting to let go. I knew that the next few months were going to be tough, but we were determined to make it through together, even if we were miles apart.

During Tony's six-month deployment, I struggled with the pain of his absence, but my children and I did our best to stay busy. Even though he was far away, we made it a point to communicate regularly and share our deepest hopes and dreams for our future together. This deployment was different from the last because we had a newfound sense of hope and encouragement that kept us going.

Tony was always so loving and supportive, reminding me of the strength of our love and our unbreakable bond. As we dreamed of the day when he would return home to us, we filled our days with joy, eager to embark on a new chapter of our lives together filled with passion and purpose.

When the day finally came, my heart raced with anticipation and anxiety. The kids and I eagerly scanned the crowd, searching for any sign of Tony. Then we saw him, walking towards us with a tired but happy smile. I ran towards him, and we hugged each other tightly, feeling our hearts beating as one.

As we settled back into our daily routine, I could not help but feel grateful for every moment we had as a family. Although we knew that Tony's deployment was just a part of our military life, we were determined to make the most of our time together. Despite the challenges, our love grew stronger with each passing day, and I knew that we could weather any storm as long as we were together.

Okinawa Japan: July 2004-June 2010

I still remember the day like it was yesterday - Tony and I received orders to Okinawa, Japan in July of 2004. A mix of excitement and fear overwhelmed me. I had never left the United States before, and the thought of starting anew in a foreign country was intimidating. Tony's love and our shared sense of adventure kept us moving forward.

As we talked about the possibilities of our upcoming journey, I felt a rush of happiness. The idea of exploring the beauty of Japan with the love of my life by my side filled me with excitement. We knew that this next adventure was going to be a challenge, but we were ready to face it together. Leaving everything we knew behind was dramatic, but the inspiration of starting a new life with Tony gave me the strength to take that leap of faith. Our love was the foundation for the new life we were about to build in Japan, and I was ready for anything that lay ahead.

Leaving Camp Lejeune was exciting for me. I was happy to leave behind all the chaos and turmoil that had been a constant part of my life for the past five years. The prospect of starting anew in a fresh and exciting place was exhilarating. Tony and I were in a wonderful place in our relationship, and I was determined to keep the momentum going.

After we received our orders, we went back to Cincinnati to say our goodbyes to family and friends. It was a tough moment for us, knowing we were going to be so far away from our loved ones. However, we were determined to make the most of our new adventure. As we hugged our family and friends, I felt a mixture of sadness and anticipation. Saying goodbye to loved ones is never easy, but we were excited about what the future held for us.

Tony and I embraced tightly, feeling grateful for the love that had brought us this far. Our four young children ages nine, seven, five, and almost four-year-old were filled with a mixture of excitement and nervousness as we embarked on our first international flight together. Our kids had never flown on an airplane before. Despite the uncertainties and challenges ahead, we were determined to start this new chapter of our lives in Okinawa. Fate had a different plan for us. Midway through our journey, one of the plane's tires blew out, forcing an unexpected landing in South Korea. The anxiety and tension in the air were frightening, but as a family, we rallied together, found our courage, and made the most of the unexpected detour.

Despite the setback, we discovered new moments of joy and excitement in the city of Osan, South Korea. We explored the vibrant streets and alleys, tried new foods, and marveled at the rich culture and history of this foreign land. We learned to navigate the challenges of language barriers and cultural differences together and found that the experience brought us even closer as a family.

Finally, we arrived in Okinawa, Japan, four days later and the heat and humidity of July enveloped us. As we stepped out of the airport, the sights, sounds, and smells of this new land overwhelmed us. The buildings, street signs, driving on the opposite side of the road, and even the food were all so different from what we were accustomed to. It was a big adjustment, but Tony and I knew that we were in it together. As we settled into the hotel, I could not help but feel a surge of gratitude at how far we had come. Our love had brought us here, at twenty-seven years old and a thousand miles away from everything and everyone we knew, to embark on a new adventure in a foreign land.

The first few weeks in Okinawa were filled with new discoveries and challenges. We had to navigate a new language, customs, and culture. It was a huge adjustment for our family, but we were determined to make the most of this opportunity. The Japanese people were friendly and welcoming, and we quickly learned to communicate to through gestures and smiles. We were amazed by the beauty of the island, with the beautiful blue skies, crystal-clear waters, and stunning beaches. We spent weekends exploring the island, taking in the local sights, and enjoying the unique cuisine.

After spending a long and exhausting month living in a hotel room, my family and I were more than eager to get a house on base. Finally, we got the call that a four-bedroom house was available. As we walked through the empty rooms, we envisioned where each of our belongings would go and how we would decorate the space to reflect our personalities and love for each other.

When we finally moved in, it was a flurry of activity as we unpacked boxes, hung up pictures and decorated every nook and cranny of our new home. Seeing my children's excited faces as they explored their new rooms filled my heart with joy. I remember the moment when we sat together in the living room, surrounded by the memories we had brought with us from our previous home, and I realized that home was not a physical place, but rather the people and memories that fill it.

With our new home in Okinawa, we were excited to start a new chapter in our lives and create new memories together. Our children were also eager to begin their new journey in this foreign land, starting school and exploring their new surroundings. Brianna was excited to start fourth grade, Kayla was looking forward to making new friends in 2nd grade, Courtney was excited to start Kindergarten, and Anthony Jr. was happy to attend full-time Head Start at the elementary school. I was happy to have all the kids in school full time.

As we settled into our new home and routines, we were filled with a sense of joy and comfort. With our family together and our home filled with love, we were ready to face anything that life in Okinawa had in store for us.

Settling In

As time went by, we settled into our new home and made friends with other military families. Our children attended school on base, and we became part of a close-knit community. Tony and I continued to work on our relationship and support each other through the ups and downs of military life. We had a new appreciation for the strength of our bond and the love that had brought us this far.

Brianna, Kayla, Courtney, and Anthony Jr were enjoying their new school and making friends with other military kids. The school and local community had a supportive environment and provided the children with ample opportunities to explore their interests. The kids participated in youth sports. They joined the soccer team, cheerleading squad, and participated in culture programs in school. Courtney started piano lessons with her kindergarten teacher. Anthony Jr. played soccer and basketball too. Seeing our children thriving brought a sense of fulfillment and pride to our hearts, knowing that we were providing them with a life full of opportunities and adventures.

We found time to explore the island's beauty and culture, from visiting Shuri Castle, American Village, Pineapple Park, Churaumi Aquarium, and attending cultural festivals to indulging in local cuisine.

I could not help but feel grateful for the island's safety and cleanliness. The beautiful beaches, parks, and landmarks were well-maintained, making it a beautiful place to raise a family. The community of military families and locals were welcoming and supportive, creating a sense of belonging and comfort that we never knew we needed. Overall, our life in Okinawa was filled with joy, adventure, and the love of family and community.

As the kids settled into their new school routine, I found myself with newfound free time during the day and a yearning for something more. That is when I discovered the joy of volunteering at the kids' elementary school. At first, it was just a way to fill my time, but I quickly realized how much I loved being around the kids, helping with activities, and teaching them new skills. Whether it was playing at recess, helping with a lesson, or reading a story during story time, I felt like I was making a difference in their lives, no matter how small. As I got more involved, I even started a weekly cooking class for Anthony Jr's class. Seeing the kids' faces light up as they learned how to mix ingredients and bake delicious treats was truly heartwarming.

Volunteering was not just about finding something to do during the day. It was also a way for me to connect with the community and make new friends. I met parents from my neighborhood who were also looking to make a difference, and we bonded over our shared experiences and goals. My friends and I joined the school's PTO program. Together, we organized events and fundraisers to support the school and its programs, and it was amazing to see how much impact a small group of dedicated volunteers could make.

Volunteering also helped me discover a newfound sense of purpose and fulfillment. It was a chance to step outside of my comfort zone and try something new, and I was amazed at how much I enjoyed it. Whether I was helping a struggling student with their math homework or organizing a school-wide field day, I felt like I was making a difference in the lives of those around me. It was a reminder that sometimes the most rewarding experiences in life come from taking a chance and giving back to others.

Tony and I continued to work on our relationship and support each other through the difficulties of military life. We had a new appreciation for the strength of our bond and the love that had brought us this far. We started to become a close-knit family who did everything together. It was everything that I always wanted.

Looking back on our time in Okinawa, I realize that it was another significant turning point in our lives. We learned to embrace change, take risks, and adapt to new circumstances. We discovered a new part of the world and made lifelong friends. Most importantly, we grew as individuals and as a family, building a foundation of resilience and love that has carried us through many more adventures and challenges. Okinawa was our saving grace.

Church Life

As a parent, seeing your kids make new friends and finding joy in new experiences is always heartwarming. That is why when our kids started attending church with our neighbors, we could not help but feel happy for them. They would come home each week with stories of new friends they had made, and the exciting activities in which they had participated.

With Easter fast approaching, our neighbors invited us to join them for a service at the church, which was conveniently located just a stone's throw from our house. As we sat in the pew listening to the sermon, I could not help but feel a sense of peace and comfort. The community at this church was welcoming and inclusive, and we could sense the love and support radiating throughout the room.

Tony and I had discussed getting more involved in church before, but we were not quite sure where to start. It was important to us because when Tony was growing up, he went to church and church camp, and I went to church on occasion and went to Vacation Bible School every summer. We knew it was something we wanted for our family, but we needed guidance. As we sat there, I realized that sometimes, the things we need are right in front of us - we just need to take that first step. Seeing our kids take the lead and embrace this new community was a reminder that it was time for us to do the same.

After the service, we chatted with some of the friendly church members and learned about the various programs and events they offered. We left feeling grateful and excited for the new journey we were about to embark on as a family. Sometimes, it is the simple things - like attending church with your loved ones - that can bring the most joy and fulfillment to our lives.

As we left the service that day, Tony and I knew that it was time for us to take the lead in making our family everything we had ever dreamed about. Our children had been the glue that held us together, and now we were inspired to deepen our faith and become even stronger as a family.

It is funny how much our children can teach us. Their innocent curiosity and boundless energy remind us of the joy in the simple things in life. Their laughter is contagious and brings us together in a way that nothing else can. We have learned that it is often the smallest things that have the biggest impact on our lives. For us, it was our kids leading us back to church that reignited our faith and brought us closer together as a family. We are grateful for their influence in our lives and for the reminder that there is something greater than ourselves to believe in.

Rediscovering our faith and finding a supportive community had a profound impact on our lives. After our first church service, Tony and I knew we wanted to make attending church a regular part of our lives. We started going every Sunday and even joined Bible Study on Wednesdays. The friendships we made were invaluable, but the greatest blessing of all was rediscovering the love we had for each other.

With the support of our church family, we made a conscious effort to work on our marriage and become better individuals. We learned to communicate more openly and to prioritize our relationship, not just for ourselves but for our family. The love and support we received from our church community helped us see the beauty in each other once again, and our love grew stronger with each passing day.

As we continued to attend church and get involved in community outreach projects, we were inspired to live a life of purpose, to put God and family first, and to give back to our community. We were amazed at how finding a community of like-minded people transformed our lives. The friendships we made, the lessons we learned, and the love we shared all contributed to making us better individuals, parents, and partners.

It was inspiring to see how other families put God and family first, and it encouraged us to do the same. We learned that with faith, love, and perseverance, anything is possible. Our marriage was stronger than ever, and our family was thriving. It was truly a transformative experience, and we were grateful for the journey that brought us there.

Rediscovering our faith and finding a supportive community was a journey that enriched our lives in countless ways. It reminded us of the power of love and the importance of putting God and family first. We were blessed to find a community that supported us through thick and thin and helped us become the best versions of ourselves. We knew that with their love and support, we could conquer anything that came our way.

Island Life

Have you ever felt unsure about your abilities or doubted whether you were on the right path in life? That is exactly how I felt until my friends encouraged me to apply for a job at my kids' elementary school. Despite my lack of a college degree and a seven-year gap in my employment history, I mustered up the courage to apply. To my surprise, I was hired as a full-time Special Education Aide. On my first day, I was nervous, but as soon as I walked into the classroom and saw those bright little faces, my heart swelled with love. Working with kids with learning disabilities and autism was an experience like no other. Seeing their progress day after day filled me with a sense of purpose I had longed for. The job was perfect for me, allowing me to be off when my kids were off and even giving me summers off. A few years later, I was promoted to be the secretary for the Special Education Department. I never would have imagined that my hesitance would lead me to find the perfect job, one that fulfilled my heart and gave me a sense of purpose.

Our family's life was filled with endless activities, from my husband's football officiating and soccer coaching to our daughter's piano lessons. We were always on the go, whether it was for work, church, sports, or school events. Despite the busy schedule, we always were available for what mattered most - spending quality time together. One of our favorite pastimes was exploring the beautiful island we called home. We loved immersing ourselves in the local culture and taking in the breathtaking scenery, especially the crystal-clear waters of the beaches. Snorkeling together, we were awestruck by the diversity of marine life and the incredible beauty of the ocean. Another thing that brought us closer as a family was our shared love for trying new restaurants and cuisines. The flavors were so unique and delicious, we could not get enough. Even amidst the chaos of everyday life, we found joy in the simplest things, and we were grateful for every moment we spent together. Life was absolutely wonderful, and we treasured each moment we had as a family.

Being a military family was not without its challenges, but we never let them get in the way of our love and commitment to each other. When Tony was away on field exercises and training missions in different countries, it was tough, but we found ways to stay connected. We wrote letters and Skyped whenever possible. I would tell him about the little things that happened in our daily lives, and he would share his experiences with us. We found joy in hearing each other's voices and seeing each other's faces, even if it was only through a computer screen.

As a family, we learned to lean on each other for support during these times of separation. We had a newfound appreciation for the time we had together and made the most of it. When Tony returned, we would run to him with open arms, happy tears streaming down our faces. We cherished every moment, making memories that would last a lifetime.

Despite the challenges that came with military life, we found that our love and commitment to each other only grew stronger with each passing day. We learned to value the time we had together and to never take each other for granted. Being a military family was not easy, but it was worth it for the love we shared.

After years of struggling through difficulties, our marriage had finally found stability, and it felt like we were more in love than ever before. We had grown closer than we ever thought possible, and it was as if we had rediscovered each other in a new light. Our determination to create the family we had always wanted, one filled with love and support, was finally paying off. The time we had spent alone together had been crucial for strengthening our bond, and we had learned to communicate better, to listen more deeply, and to appreciate each other for who we truly were. Our faith in God and our participation in church activities had also played a crucial role in building a solid foundation for our family, and we had found lifelong friends who inspired us to keep going and to never give up. We saw firsthand how love and commitment could stand the test of time through their examples, and it gave us hope and a sense of purpose. Every day that passed, our bond grew stronger, and we knew that together, we could conquer anything life throws our way. We were grateful for the love and support we had found in each other, and for the beautiful family we were building together, one filled with hope, joy, and unwavering devotion.

Our love for Okinawa, Japan was like no other. It was a love that made us feel alive, and it compelled us to extend our orders for another three years. Six years in total, and it still felt like we had just arrived yesterday. Living on this tiny island felt like living in a fairytale world, where every day was an adventure waiting to happen. We were cocooned in our little bubble of happiness, where we could be ourselves without a care in the world. The people were welcoming, the food was delicious, and the scenery was breathtaking. We explored every inch of the island, from the breathtaking landscapes to the clear waters of the ocean. We hiked the rugged terrains, swam with tropical fish, and discovered hidden beaches that seemed straight out of a dream. The vibrant culture of Okinawa was also a delight to experience, with its unique music, dance, and cuisine. The time we spent together as a family was the most precious thing of all, and it was a joy to watch our children grow up surrounded by such beauty and wonder. Our love for each other only grew stronger with each passing day, and as we looked out at the vast Pacific Ocean, we knew that we were exactly where we were meant to be. Our time in Okinawa was a gift that we would always cherish, a reminder that true happiness comes not from material possessions but from the simple joys of life and the love we share with those closest to our hearts.

Saying Goodbye

As our time in Okinawa was ending, we were filled with a mix of nervousness and excitement about returning to the States. Saying goodbye to the place we had called home for the last six years was hard. We were sad to leave the beautiful island of Okinawa behind, but excited to embark on a new chapter in our lives. Our family had grown so much during our time there. Our kids were now fifteen, thirteen, twelve, and almost ten years old.

We had immersed ourselves in the culture and learned so much about ourselves and each other. We had learned to cherish every moment together, and to make the most of our time as a family. We had discovered new hobbies and interests, and created countless happy memories that we would always treasure. From playing games and sports outside, to listening to music and singing karaoke, to cooking and hosting parties with friends, we had become the family we had always wanted to be.

We had created a life of joy and love in this magical place, where our children had thrived and our bonds with friends had grown stronger than ever. The island had become our little slice of paradise, where we cherished every moment together and learned to appreciate the simple things in life. We had discovered a world of wonder and beauty that we would always cherish.

As we packed our bags and said our goodbyes, we knew that Okinawa had left an indelible mark on our hearts. It was here that we had found God and built a solid foundation for our family, one that would see us through any challenge that lay ahead. It was here that we had forged lifelong friendships, relationships that had grown so close that our friends had become our family. It was here that we had learned to appreciate the moments we shared with each other, to be present and fully engaged in each other's lives.

As we looked back on our time in Okinawa, we were filled with gratitude for the experiences we had shared and the memories we had made. From exploring unfamiliar places and trying new things to hosting parties and spending lazy afternoons at the beach, every moment had been a precious gift. While we were sad to leave, we knew that our time in Okinawa had prepared us for the adventures and challenges that were ahead. Our family bond was unbreakable, forged through the experiences and memories we shared. We were excited to create new memories and discover new places, but we would always carry Okinawa with us, a source of inspiration, love, resilience, and comfort wherever we went.

Twenty-Nine Palms California: June 2010-June 2013

Leaving the beauty and comfort of Okinawa was not going to be easy. We could not help but feel a twinge of apprehension about what lay ahead. Our next duty station was in Twenty-Nine Palms, CA and our family was determined to make the most of our new surroundings. The stark desert landscape presented a stark contrast to the beautiful beaches of Okinawa, and at first, it felt unfamiliar and foreboding. However, we were not ones to back down from a challenge. With a sense of adventure and curiosity, we set out to explore our new home, eager to discover all the hidden treasures it had to offer.

We started exploring our surroundings and discovered some hidden gems in the desert, like hiking trails and beautiful parks like Joshua Tree. The harsh desert climate was a clear contrast to the idyllic island paradise. We marveled at the beauty of the desert landscape, discovering new sights and sounds that we had never experienced before. We soon learned to appreciate the unique qualities that made the desert such a special place.

Of course, the transition was not without its challenges. The hot, dry heat proved to be a major adjustment, and Anthony Jr. frequently suffered from nosebleeds. The kids struggled to adjust to their new schools and the lack of familiar faces, but with our support and encouragement, they soon found their footing. We immersed ourselves in the activities offered on base, from bowling to swimming to catching a movie, and slowly but surely, we began to feel at home.

As a family of faith, finding a church community was important to us, but we struggled to find the right fit. Despite this, we remained optimistic, confident that we would eventually find our place in this new community. With our love and support for one another, and our unwavering trust in God's plan, we knew that we could overcome any obstacle and thrive in this new environment.

Starting a new life in the harsh desert climate of Twenty-Nine Palms was no easy feat, but our family took it in stride. We quickly found a place to call home on base housing and enrolled our children in school, with Brianna in tenth grade, Kayla in eighth grade, and Courtney and Anthony Jr in fifth and sixth grade. The transition was not without its challenges, but we were grateful for some familiar faces our children found in their new school. As we settled into our new routine, we marveled at the stunning sunsets and the unique beauty of our surroundings. It was a different kind of paradise, but we learned to see the beauty in it.

After six months of adjusting to our new life, I found a part-time job as a Special Education Aide at my children's elementary school on base. It was a perfect fit for our family's schedule, and I was excited to be back in a routine and working again. Being busy and productive helped me to feel more settled and at ease in our new home. Despite the challenges of starting over in a new place, we were grateful for the opportunities it presented, and for the chance to make new memories as a family.

Twenty-Nine Palms is a small town with nothing much to do, but that did not stop us from making the most out of our long weekends. We eagerly set out to explore the surrounding areas. We would often take long road trips to nearby cities like San Diego, LA, Palm Springs, and even Las Vegas, to soak in the sights and sounds of these vibrant locations. Our trips were filled with adventure and excitement as we visited zoos, beaches, and amusement parks, and created unforgettable memories along the way. The cameras were always out, capturing every moment so that we could look back on them with fondness and nostalgia.

Our family bond remained strong, and we were there to support each other through the difficulties. Whether it was the kid's soccer games or Anthony Jr's basketball games, we were always in attendance, cheering them on every step of the way.

As a family, we made sure to prioritize spending quality time together, and we enjoyed many game nights, movie nights, and family dinners. We loved and supported each other, and that was the foundation that kept us strong. We were each other's rock, and the love we had for one another was a force that kept us going, even on the toughest of days.

Deployment to Okinawa Japan: June 2011-Dec. 2011

Life has a funny way of surprising us, and sometimes, it is in unexpected ways. Just a year after leaving our beloved Okinawa behind, Tony, got deployed back there for six months on the 31st MEU.

It was a challenging time for our family as we were still adjusting to our new life in California, and we missed Tony terribly. I could not help but feel a tinge of envy as he got to see our friends and visit our favorite spots. However, we managed to soldier on despite the distance and kept ourselves busy with the kids' activities and daily routines.

Amidst the hardship, a glimmer of hope shone through. We were delighted to find out that some of the families we knew from Okinawa had also made the move to California. Reuniting with old friends was a welcome respite for our family, and we cherished the time spent together. It was a reminder that even during tough times, there are silver linings to be found and cherished.

Thankfully, our old next-door neighbors from Okinawa were stationed in Twenty-Nine Palms too, and they moved into base housing just a few streets over from us. I cannot even describe how thrilled we were to have them near us again. Our kids were great friends, and it was a huge relief to have someone to spend time with while Tony was away. Her husband also was deployed with Tony. So, our families spent a lot of time together. It was a fantastic way to pass the time. We created new memories, had lots of laughs, went to drive inn movies, played lots of fun board games, and forged a bond that would last a lifetime.

After what felt like an eternity, Tony finally came home from his deployment right before Christmas. The excitement was noticeable in the air, and the kids could not contain their joy. We were thrilled to be reunited as a family once again.

For a family getaway, we took our kids to Disneyland for the holidays, and it was a magical experience for all of us. We went on rides, took pictures with our favorite Disney characters, and watched the spectacular parade of lights. It was a much-needed break from our daily routine and a reminder that even in the toughest of times, there is always something to look forward to.

The experience taught us that with the love and support of our family and friends, we could overcome any obstacle that life throws our way. We were grateful for the time we spent apart because it made us appreciate each other even more.

Deployment to Afghanistan: Sept. 2012-April 2013

Another deployment, this time to Afghanistan. I was scared beyond measure. We were still in the midst of a war, and people were still dying. My biggest fear was losing Tony. Every day, I prayed for his safety and that of his fellow Marines.

Communication became our lifeline during that deployment. My husband and I were separated by thousands of miles, but we found ways to stay connected. We emailed each other constantly, FaceTime whenever he could, and sent care packages filled with goodies that reminded him of home. Despite the distance, we never felt alone.

It was not easy. Being away from my husband was especially hard during Brianna's senior year of high school. She was growing up so fast, accomplishing so much, and I wanted him to be there for every milestone. She got her driver's license, had a part-time job, was the captain of her soccer team, and even had her first boyfriend. It was bittersweet watching her grow up so quickly, but every time I missed him, I held onto the hope that we would all be together again.

Even thought it was ones the toughest thing I have ever had to do - being a military wife and raising our family while my husband was deployed. I knew I had to be strong for the rest of us. So, I dug deep, finding strength in my faith and in the love that Tony and I shared.

During those long months apart, I learned to appreciate the little things that made up our lives. I savored every soccer game, every school play, and every family dinner, knowing that each one was a precious moment that we could not get back. It was not always easy, with Tony missing birthdays, holidays, and different activities but I was determined to make the most of the time we had.

Tony's love for me was my lifeline during those dark times. Even when he was thousands of miles away, his words and actions made me feel connected to him in a way that transcended distance. His love gave me hope and motivation to keep going, even when things seemed dreary.

This deployment was especially challenging for me. Our kids were older, with their own lives and schedules, and it was harder to keep everyone on the same page. Brianna's rebellious behavior was escalating. She was sneaking out to see her boyfriend, lying about where she was, and pushing me away. Tensions were high, and it was hard to know how to bring our family back together.

Through it all, Tony was my rock. He offered unwavering support and love from afar, reminding me that we were in this together. Even with his help, it was exhausting doing everything on my own. I tried to keep our family together while he was away, juggling work, kids, and household duties all at once. It was a constant balancing act, and I often felt like I was on the brink of falling apart. I could not wait to have Tony home safe and sound.

Then, in April 2013, Tony and his fellow Marines finally returned home safely. I will never forget the feeling of pure joy and relief when I saw him walking off the bus. We were finally reunited, and our family was whole again. Tony was able to witness Brianna's graduation from high school in May and be a part of our kids' lives once more.

In the end, I came out of this deployment with a new appreciation for the fragility and beauty of life. I learned that every moment counts, and that the love of family is what makes it all worthwhile.

As time went on, I noticed a change in Tony. He was different - distant, always on edge, hyper vigilant, and quick to anger. I knew something was wrong, but he was hesitant to talk about it. I believed he was suffering from PTSD. As a Marine, he believed in toughing it out and dealing with things on his own. I refused to let him suffer in silence. I reminded him that he was not alone, that he had a family who loved him and friends who cared about him. Tony never had a problem talking to me about the things that happened over in Afghanistan. The problem was that he was always on edge and quick to anger. That was not like him at all. Tony has aways been so easy going and relaxed.

It was a tough journey, but I encouraged him to seek counseling and talk about what he was going through. I told him it was not a sign of weakness but rather a sign of strength. It was not easy - there were moments of frustration, anger, and despair. But with patience, love, and understanding, we navigated through it together.

Through it all, I realized the true power of love and commitment. Even when things got tough, we stuck together and never gave up. Tony's strength and resilience inspired me to be the best version of myself. We faced many challenges, but we never lost sight of what was most important - our love for each other and our family.

In the end, our commitment to each other and our willingness to seek help and support made all the difference. Tony learned that it is okay to ask for help and that seeking counseling is not a sign of weakness. We emerged from that challenging time stronger and more in love than ever before.

As our time in Twenty-Nine Palms was ending, we could not wait to see where our next set of orders would take us. The dry desert had been our home for the past three years, but it was time to start a new adventure. We did not have many options for entertainment, but that did not stop us from making the most of our time there.

Our home may have been modest, but it was filled with love and warmth. We had countless movie and bowling nights on base, and we loved visiting the off-base Drive-Inn movie theater and Lucky Park. We always found ways to have fun and make memories together.

As we started packing up our belongings, I felt a mix of emotions. I was sad to leave my job and the friends I had made, but I was excited for the next chapter. I was going to miss the breathtaking desert sunrises and sunsets, but I knew that we would be making new memories soon enough.

With each box we packed and each goodbye we said, our love grows stronger. No matter where the military took us, we knew that we had each other. We were ready for whatever came next, and I could not wait to see what the future held for us.

Murrieta California: June 2013-June 2015

When Tony received orders in June 2013 to Miramar, California in San Diego, we were over the moon with excitement! Finally, we were leaving the blistering desert behind and moving to a place we absolutely loved. The thought of being able to go to the beach, enjoy the temperate weather, and explore the endless attractions San Diego had to offer filled us with anticipation.

After careful consideration, we decided to take the plunge and buy our very first house in Murrieta, California, which was about an hour from Tony's work. The house was perfect for us with an inground pool in the backyard to cool off in and enough bedrooms for all the kids to have their own room. The house was beautiful, and it felt like a dream come true.

Although the commute was long for Tony, we were determined to make it work. We wanted to provide stability for our children and give them a sense of belonging. Moving during the teenage years can be incredibly tough, so we made sure that our kids could stay in one high school and graduate together with their friends. We wanted them to have the opportunity to create lasting memories and form strong friendships.

As we settled into our new home in Murrieta, we could not help but feel a sense of pride and accomplishment. We had come a long way from our humble beginnings and had overcome so many challenges together. From living in the projects, Tony's deployments to raising our children, we had been through a lot, but we had always remained steadfast in our commitment to our family.

Our new home represented more than just a roof over our heads. It was a symbol of our resilience, our love, and our dedication to building a better life for ourselves and our family. We were excited to take on the task of making it our own, starting with a fresh coat of paint and some much-needed DIY projects around the house.

As we tackled each task, we appreciated every moment and savored the time we spent together. It was a reminder that we could overcome any obstacle that came our way as long as we were together. The house became a canvas for us to express our creativity and love for one another.

In the end, our new home in Murrieta became more than just a physical space. It became a place where we could grow, laugh, and create lasting memories. We were grateful for the opportunity to start a new chapter in our lives and to be able to share it with each other.

Time was moving faster than ever for our family. Our children were growing up right before our eyes, and it was both exciting and bittersweet. Brianna had recently graduated from high school in Twenty-Nine Palms and was feeling uncertain about her future. She had always been an ambitious person, but she was struggling to find her place in the world. Despite her uncertainty, she was determined to keep moving forward. She got a job and enrolled in community college to explore her options.

Kayla was also making strides in her academics. She was attending eleventh grade and working part-time to save up for college. Meanwhile, Courtney was navigating the challenges of freshman year at the same school as Kayla. Anthony Jr was in eighth grade at the local junior high, eager to make new friends and explore new opportunities.

As parents, we were proud to see our children thriving in their new schools and making meaningful connections with their peers. It was a testament to their resilience and adaptability. We were determined to support them in any way we could and encourage them to pursue their passions.

As a family, we were determined to make the most of our new chapter in Murrieta. We explored the local parks, visited the beach on weekends, and spent quality time together. Even though life was busy, we made it a priority to cherish the little moments and appreciate the beauty around us. Our new home had given us the chance to start anew and build a life full of hope and promise.

Tony missed officiating football. He was gone a lot when we lived in Twenty-Nine Palms, so he did not get to officiate often. He was excited to get back at it. He started officiating high school football games and youth football on the weekends, relishing the opportunity to be a part of the action and make a little extra money for our family.

Football had always been a passion of Tony's. Tony loves everything football, to youth, high school, college, and NFL. His favorite team is the Cincinnati Bengals. He also loves the camaraderie and thrill of being on the field. He relishes the chance to connect with other fans and officials and to share his knowledge and expertise with the younger players.

Despite our family's success in adapting to our new life in Murrieta, I struggled to find work. I had my heart set on working at an elementary school, but my lack of a college degree seemed to be a barrier. It was discouraging to receive repeated rejections, but I tried not to let it get me down. Instead, I focused on using my time off to work on our home improvement projects, going to the gym, and enjoying our beautiful pool.

As the family's go-to chauffeur, I spent a lot of time shuttling the kids to and from school and all their various activities. It was a hectic schedule, but I appreciated the opportunity to be there for them and support their interests. I watched proudly as Brianna worked hard to find her path, Kayla pursued her academics while working part-time, and Courtney blossomed into a confident young woman. Anthony Jr. continued to make friends and play sports all year around.

Although it would have been nice to have a job, I was grateful for the break and the chance to focus on our family and home. I used the extra time to dive deeper into my hobbies and passions, such as cooking, Do- It -Yourself projects, and crafting. It was a reminder that life is full of unexpected twists and turns, and sometimes the best thing we can do is embrace the moment and enjoy the journey.

Our family had established our new life in Murrieta, and we were all enjoying our beautiful home and the wonderful community around us. So, when we received the surprising news that Tony had received orders to Camp Pendleton in October of 2014, we were caught off guard but also grateful for the opportunity to stay put and maintain some normalcy.

Despite the unexpected nature of the orders, we were thrilled to be able to continue living in our dream home and watching our children thrive in their new community and schools. Tony's commute to Camp Pendleton was shorter, which was a welcome relief from his previous long drive. We all felt a sense of stability and security in our home, which had become a symbol of our family's resilience and love. The kids were especially thrilled about the prospect of staying in their home and maintaining their friendships. They had taken immense pride in decorating and painting their own rooms, and they loved nothing more than spending time in the pool on hot summer afternoons. As a family, we had created a sanctuary in Murrieta, and we were grateful for the chance to continue building our lives there.

June 2015 was a momentous time for our family. Kayla, our second oldest, was graduating from high school and heading off to college in New York City. She was accepted into St. John's University. We were bursting with pride as we watched her achieve her dreams and work hard to make them a reality. Seeing her success was a powerful reminder that with hard work and determination, anything is possible.

As excited as we were for Kayla's next chapter, we could not help but feel a bit of sadness as we prepared to say goodbye. We knew we were going to miss her terribly when she moved across the country to a place she had never been before. We also knew that she was destined for remarkable things, and we were grateful to have had the chance to watch her grow and flourish.

Meanwhile, Courtney was wrapping up her tenth-grade year with excellence, and Anthony Jr. was thriving both academically and athletically. As a family, we continued to support each other through all of life's difficulties, celebrating each other's triumphs and providing comfort and encouragement during the tough times. Brianna, our oldest, was still living at home and working, trying to figure out her own passions and goals. While we knew she was struggling to find her path, we also knew that she had the same determination and drive as the rest of our family, and we were confident that she would find her way in time.

As a military family, unexpected orders were always a possibility, but it still felt like a shock when it happened to us again. I felt like the ground was pulled out from under our feet. Moving around so frequently can be difficult for children, especially when they are settled in school and making friends. We understood how important it was for Courtney and Anthony Jr to stay in the same school and graduate with their friends. It was a stability that we wanted to provide for them, but sometimes the military had other plans.

The thought of uprooting our family once again was overwhelming. We had created a home in Murrieta and made lasting memories. We did not want to leave everything behind. How was our family going to cope with another move? We had only been in our house for two years. It felt so unfair, and the kids were going to be devastated. The thought of telling them was daunting but we knew we had to face it as a family.

Quantico Virginia: June 2015- October 2020

As my husband Tony and I sat down with our children, Courtney, and Anthony Jr., to tell them about the military's unexpected orders to Quantico, VA, our hearts sank. We had only been in our house in Murrieta, CA for two years, and the thought of uprooting our family once again was terrifying.

Instead of wallowing in despair, we decided to look for the silver linings. Tony and I reminded each other of the exciting adventures we have had as a military family and all the new places we've experienced together. We agreed to approach this move as an opportunity for growth and new experiences, and not to focus on the negative.

When we broke the news to Courtney and Anthony Jr., they were understandably upset and cried. They had both been excelling in school, making friends, and planning to graduate with their classmates. Tony and I reassured them that we would make the best of the situation and find new things to love about our next location. We promised them that we would face this challenge together as a family, and that we would do everything we could to make the transition as smooth as possible.

Meanwhile, our daughter Kayla was thrilled about the move. She had just graduated high school and was accepted to St. John's College in New York City and was eager to start her next adventure on the East Coast.

Our oldest daughter Brianna, however, was not thrilled about the move. She was adamant she was going to stay in California and find her own path. While we respected her decision, we also knew that it would be extremely hard for her.

Despite the uncertainty and anxiety that came with this sudden move, we were determined to embrace it as an opportunity for growth and new experiences. Our family dynamics were going to change but we promised to support each other and make the transition as smooth as possible.

As a family, we embarked on a bittersweet journey of preparing for our move across the country. Tony and I knew that selling our beautiful home was the best decision, even though it tugged at our heartstrings. As we packed up our memories and prepared for the move, we found solace in the excitement of starting a new chapter in our lives.

As the final boxes were packed and our beloved home in Murrieta sold, our family embarked on a bittersweet journey to a new chapter in our lives. Brianna, our 20-year-old daughter, decided to move in with Tony's sister in San Diego while working and attending community college. After completing high school, Kayla was ready to see the world. With a passion for adventure, she spent most of the summer exploring through Europe. Our other children Courtney and Anthony Jr finished their school year, we decided to take advantage of the summer and make the move to our new home in Quantico, Virginia a memorable experience.

Rather than take the easy route and fly, we decided to pack up the car and make it a family road trip. Along the way, we made many stops to visit friends and family, and even took detours to some of the country's most famous landmarks. These were moments that our family would treasure forever and made leaving California a little easier.

As we arrived in Quantico, we were greeted by the lush greenery and rolling hills of Virginia. The excitement of exploring our new area filled us with energy, and we could not wait to see what adventures awaited us. Despite the initial sadness of leaving our old life behind, we knew that our family was ready for this new opportunity, and we were determined to make the most of it.

It did not take us long to settle into our new home in Virginia. We were fortunate enough to secure base housing quickly, and our new house was spacious enough to accommodate our entire family. The best part was that the community pool was just a few steps away from our backyard, so we spent a lot of time there during the summer months.

As we explored our new surroundings both on and off base, we had some incredible adventures. One of our most memorable experiences was visiting Washington DC, which was only a short 45-minute drive away. We marveled at the iconic monuments and soaked up all the knowledge we could at the city's many museums.

Our travels also took us to New York, where we helped our daughter Kayla settle into St. John's College. Although it was hard to say goodbye to her, we were excited for the opportunities that awaited her. Leaving her in the big city was bittersweet, and we could not help but feel a bit sad as our family of six was reduced to just four, with Brianna staying in California and Kayla starting a new chapter in her life. Despite this change, we remained optimistic and inspired to make the most of our time together as a family.

Life Goes On

The start of the new school year brought a wave of excitement and nervousness for our family as our two teenagers began their high school journey on base. Courtney was in the 11th grade and Anthony Jr was in the 10th grade. As we walked through the halls on the first day of school, I could see the apprehension in their eyes as they looked around at their new environment. It was a stark contrast from their previous school in California, with only a fraction of the students and activities available to them. Their old school in Murrieta had about 1,000 students per grade and now their new school had only 20-30 students per grade. Their new high school was also a middle school with grades sixth- twelfth. Everything was completely different.

Anthony Jr was especially anxious, having been a popular and active student in his previous school. He missed the sports teams, school sponsored events and programs, and other extracurricular activities he used to participate in. We tried to encourage him to find new interests and activities to pursue, but he remained disappointed. Meanwhile, Courtney adapted quickly to the change, finding solace in the smaller, more intimate atmosphere of her new school. She made new friends easily and enjoyed the more personalized attention from her teachers.

As parents, we felt a mix of pride and worry for our children. We wanted them to succeed and thrive in their new environment, but we also knew it would be a challenging adjustment for them. Nonetheless, we remained optimistic and supported them as best we could, encouraging them to embrace new experiences and opportunities. We were excited to see how their high school journey would unfold and the unique memories they would create along the way.

As we adjusted to life in Virginia, we all found ourselves facing new challenges and opportunities. Our children, Courtney, and Anthony Jr were navigating their high school experience in a smaller school setting. Anthony Jr struggled initially, missing the excitement of competing in high level sports and participating in various activities. He was not one to sit idly by. He took the initiative and joined the school sports teams, playing year-round and making new friends in the process. Meanwhile, Courtney found comfort in the slower pace of things. They both started getting involved in various school activities, including hosting dances, helping new students, and participating in school plays and sports. I was very thankful that they had each other.

As I watched my children adapt to change, I began to feel the pull of something new for myself. I had missed working with children and decided to apply to a local elementary school as a Special Education Aide. When I received the job offer, I was thrilled. It felt good to have something that was just mine, a purpose outside of being a military spouse and mother. As I began working with the children, I felt fulfilled and reinvigorated, grateful for the opportunity to make a difference in their lives. It was also nice to make new friends within the school community.

While balancing our family's new life in Virginia, I immersed myself in my work, attended the kids' games, and drove them around to all their different activities. Meanwhile, Tony new unit was demanding and stressful, keeping him busy and often working late.

Despite the challenges, our family continued to persevere. We were proud to watch our children grow and thrive in their unfamiliar environment and pursue their interests and passions. Adapting and adjusting to our new circumstances became second nature, and we found ways to support and encourage each other along the way.

As our children grew more independent, Tony and I started to prioritize our relationship. Despite our busy schedules, we made an effort to be available for each other, going on more date nights and trying new activities together. Cooking became one of our favorite shared hobbies. We loved experimenting with new recipes and trying unusual flavor combinations. We loved different cuisines, from Italian to Japanese to Indian, and challenging ourselves to recreate our favorite restaurant dishes at home. Grilling and smoking different meats was another one of our passions. We enjoyed making our own rubs and sauces. We liked trying different flavor profiles on meats. We also loved watching cooking and barbeque shows on tv to get inspiration from.

Through our shared love of cooking, we not only deepened our connection as a couple but also found a way to bring our family and friends together. Hosting dinner parties and barbecues became a regular occurrence, and we relished in the joy of sharing our creations with our loved ones. Our kitchen became the heart of our home, where we laughed, bonded, and created cherished memories that we still look back on fondly to this day.

Traveling and exploring unfamiliar places was something we enjoyed as a couple, and we also discovered a mutual love for woodworking. Starting with a simple farmhouse table, we found ourselves hooked on the process of creating beautiful and functional pieces from scratch. Woodworking was a wonderful way to spend time together, and the joy we found in working together was immeasurable. As our woodworking skills improved, we tackled more complex projects, like building a game cabinet and designing custom furniture. The process of planning, measuring, and cutting wood became a therapeutic and bonding experience for us. We spent hours discussing our ideas and making sure we were on the same page, often adjusting and making improvising along the way.

Through our shared hobbies and experiences, Tony and I gained a deeper understanding of each other. We discovered how we approach problem-solving and our unique styles of learning. These insights helped us communicate better and strengthened our relationship.

As we continued to explore our interests, we found that they not only brought us closer together but also allowed us to grow individually. We were constantly learning new skills, discovering new hobbies, and pushing ourselves outside of our comfort zones.

Tony also found ways to reconnect with his personal passions, both old and new. He resumed officiating high school and youth football, and returned to fishing, a beloved pastime from his childhood. Being out on the water and catching fish brought him a sense of peace and happiness. He was thrilled when he finally saved up enough to purchase his own fishing boat and spent countless hours exploring the local lakes and rivers. Even the kids loved to join him on these adventures, bonding over the thrill of the catch and the beauty of nature.

For me, finding joy in the little things was important. I loved creating photo books of our adventures, reliving the memories, and cherishing the moments we shared. Crafting was also a favorite pastime of mine, and I enjoyed using my creativity to make beautiful things. Decorating for holidays and doing fun activities with the family were other things that brought me happiness.

Playing board games was one of our favorite family activities, and I loved seeing how much fun we could have together. Being a mother and a wife was everything to me, and I found so much fulfillment in nurturing my family and watching them grow. Bringing us closer as a family was always a top priority for me, and I treasured every moment we spent together.

As our children matured, we took extraordinary pride in their independence and responsibility. Brianna's choice to return home a year later was a clear indication of the tight bond we shared as a family. Her decision to follow her passion and enroll in cosmetology school was a source of inspiration for all of us. We were thrilled to have her back with us and excited to watch her grow and success.

Meanwhile, Kayla was thriving in New York, pursuing her education, working part-time, and exploring new opportunities. We were so proud of her and all that she had accomplished. She was a source of motivation for our other children, showing them that with hard work and dedication, anything is possible.

Courtney and Anthony Jr also had jobs, and they were learning the value of hard work and responsibility. We were proud of their work ethic and dedication to their jobs while going to school. As a couple, Tony and I continued to find time for each other despite our busy lives. We were always looking for new adventures to embark on together.

As we faced new challenges and embarked on new adventures, the love we had for each other as a family never wavered. We knew that the future was unpredictable, but we also knew that if we had each other's support, we could overcome any obstacle that came our way. The bond we shared was unbreakable, and it gave us the strength and resilience to face whatever lay ahead with optimism and determination.

In June of 2017, our daughter Courtney graduated from high school, marking a special moment for our family. Witnessing her take the first steps towards her future and pursue her dreams was a cause for celebration. As she began attending classes at a community college for Dental Assisting later that year, we saw her blossom into a confident and eager young woman. Meanwhile, Anthony Jr was heading into his senior year, and Brianna had graduated from Cosmetology School and was forging her own path in the world. Kayla continued to thrive in college and intern at local hospitals.

As our family members achieved their milestones, we were inspired by Tony's hard work and dedication as he graduated in 2017 with his bachelor's degree in Exercise Science. Seeing him walk across that stage filled us with immense pride and reminded us that anything is possible with perseverance and hard work. Through all the difficulties, we remained close-knit and supportive of each other, inspiring one another to pursue our dreams and never give up.

Then in June of 2018, Anthony Jr graduated from high school and earned a full ride scholarship to UMASS Dartmouth, we felt an overwhelming sense of pride and joy as parents. Witnessing our son reach such a milestone was a testament to his hard work and dedication.

Throughout our life together, Tony and I had always strived to inspire each other and our children to pursue their passions and work hard to achieve their dreams. Seeing all our children grow into independent and kind-hearted individuals filled us with immense gratitude and happiness.

As we celebrated our 20th wedding anniversary, I could not help but reflect on our journey together. Despite the challenges and triumphs, Tony had always been my unwavering rock, offering me love and support. Our love story was a testament to our unrelenting perseverance and devotion, and I was incredibly fortunate to have him as my lifelong partner. In retrospect, it was these little moments - the graduations, the festivities, the date nights, and the significant accomplishments - that fueled the growth of our love, every day.

In May of 2019, our family experienced another proud moment as Kayla graduated from St. John's University in New York City with a bachelor's degree in Radiologic Technology. Watching her receive her degree was an unforgettable moment for Tony and me, knowing all the arduous work she had put in to get there. She decided to remain in New York City and start her career at a local hospital, which we knew was an excellent opportunity for her.

In the same year, Courtney also graduated from her Dental Assistance Program and started working in a dental office, which was a field she was enthusiastic about. Anthony Jr continued to thrive in his second year at UMASS Dartmouth, and we were grateful that all our children were finding success and pursuing their passions. We continued to be amazed by Brianna's skills and creativity in her career as a hairstylist.

As we embarked on a new chapter of our lives, Tony made the difficult but wise decision to retire from the Marine Corps after twenty-two years of unwavering commitment to his country. On October 31, 2020, he laced up his boots for the last time, marking the end of an era. The decision to retire was not an easy one, but it was the right one for our family. As we searched for a new home to start our new life, we reminisced about our early days together, the challenges we faced, and the joys we experienced as a couple and as a family. Through thick and thin, we have stuck together and built a family of which we are proud.

Despite the uncertainty that comes with change, our love and trust in each other remained steadfast. Together, we visited potential homes and explored new neighborhoods, keeping our hearts and minds open to new experiences. After searching high and low, we finally found the perfect house - a spacious 3000 sq ft home on three acres of land. As we walked through the doors, we were immediately struck by the beauty and charm of the house and the surrounding landscape. It was more than just a house; it was a place where we could escape from the world and just be together.

With every stroke of the brush and every nail we hammered, we fell more in love with our new home. Together, we spent our weekends working on projects and making our house a home. Tony's expertise in construction and my eye for design made us the perfect team. From painting the walls to planting a garden, we were able to create a space that truly reflected our personalities and our love for each other.

One of our favorite things to do was to sit on the porch swing and watch the sunset. As the sun slowly disappeared behind the trees, we would hold hands and reflect on our journey together. We were grateful for the life we had built and the memories we had created. Our new home was more than just a place to live; it was a symbol of our love and commitment to each other. It was our little piece of paradise, our own private oasis, where we could escape from the world and just be together. We knew that no matter where life took us, as long as we were together, we would always feel at home.

Covid 19: March 2020

In March 2020, our lives were forever changed when the Covid-19 pandemic struck our nation with unprecedented force. The virus spread at an alarming rate, and hospitals were quickly overwhelmed, leaving healthcare workers like Kayla, a Radiologic Technologist, on the front lines of this battle. Our family's plans for a peaceful transition from military life were suddenly upended, and we were forced to confront the harsh reality of a global pandemic that threatened to engulf us all.

The ensuing days and weeks were a blur of anxiety, fear, and uncertainty as we grappled with the unknown and tried to adjust to a new way of life. Confined to our home, we felt isolated from the rest of the world, unsure of what the future held. For Kayla, the challenge was particularly unsettling as she continued to risk her health and safety by working at the hospital.

As the pandemic raged on, we were forced to adapt to a new reality. Our schools and workplaces closed, and we had to find ways to work and learn from home. The challenges were relentless, but we remained strong and resolute in our determination to persevere.

Amidst the chaos and uncertainty, we found inspiration in the selflessness of frontline workers, who risked everything to care for others. We also found comfort in our love for each other, relying on one another for support and strength.

As the weeks turned into months, we learned to appreciate the simple things in life, like cooking meals together and spending quality time as a family. Although our marriage faced new challenges as we spent every moment together, we remained committed to supporting one another and navigating this unprecedented time as a team.

Even in a world of turmoil, we discovered a hidden treasure that had been there all along: each other's company. As we spent our days confined to the house, we never once felt bored or restless. Instead, we embarked on various projects that brought us even closer together.

During the pandemic, we were fortunate to have three out of our four children back home with us. The experience was a beautiful reminder of the importance of family and togetherness in challenging times.

For the first time in years, we had the chance to hang out and connect with our children without the distractions of busy schedules and outside obligations. We spent long hours chatting, playing games, and catching up on old times. We discovered new things about our children that we had never known before, and we marveled at the incredible individuals they had become.

It was a joy to see our family reunited, to share meals, and to enjoy each other's company. We were able to bond over shared experiences, reminisce about past memories, and make new ones that we would cherish forever.

Despite the joy of having most of our children back home with us, there was a sense of longing for our daughter, Kayla, who worked tirelessly as a Radiologic Technologist at a local hospital on the front lines of the pandemic.

We missed her physical presence in the house, her infectious laughter, and her witty sense of humor. However, we knew that she was doing an incredibly important job, and we were proud of her unwavering dedication to her patients and her profession.

To stay connected, we would FaceTime with Kayla often, checking in on her, and sharing stories about our day-to-day lives. Hearing about her experiences at the hospital was both heartbreaking and inspiring. She would tell us about the struggles and challenges of working during a pandemic, but she also shared stories of hope, healing, and resilience.

Despite the distance, we felt connected to Kayla through these conversations, and we found comfort in knowing that she was doing something meaningful and impactful. We were proud of her courage and dedication, and we knew that she was making a difference in the lives of those around her.

Kayla's absence was a reminder of the sacrifices and hardships that healthcare workers were making during the pandemic. We were grateful for her bravery and for all those who were working on the front lines, risking their own lives to help others.

As the pandemic raged on outside, we found comfort in the safety of our family home. We laughed, cried, and celebrated together, reminding ourselves of the love and strength that we had as a family. We were grateful for the time we had to reconnect and deepen our family bonds, and we knew that this experience would remain with us forever.

We transformed our home into a sanctuary that reflected our personalities and tastes, painting the walls with vibrant colors that spoke to our souls and creating cozy nooks where we could cuddle up with a book and a cup of coffee. In the evenings, we danced to our favorite music, our bodies swaying in perfect harmony, and we laughed until our stomachs hurt.

Watching movies together was never a mundane experience; it was a chance to explore new worlds and create new memories. When the weather permitted, we ventured outside for movie nights under the stars, the crackling of the firepit in the background making the atmosphere even more magical.

During the day, we would take long walks, hand in hand, talking about our dreams and aspirations. The world outside might have been uncertain, but within the safety of our love, we felt grateful for the blessings we had. Our love grew stronger with each passing day, and we realized that being together was all we needed to make everything else fall into place.

In those quiet moments together, we found solace from the chaos of the world outside. We discovered the power of connection, the beauty of simplicity, and the strength of love. As we navigated the challenges of the pandemic, we were reminded that even in the darkest of times, love has the power to illuminate our path and guide us towards a brighter future.

As the summer of 2020 slowly approached, things began to open again. We emerged from our cocoon, wearing masks, and keeping our distance from others, but with a newfound appreciation for the simple things in life. As the department stores gradually started to open back up, we took the opportunity to stroll through the aisles, hand in hand, marveling at the wonders of the world around us. Although most restaurants were only offering carry-out, we made the most of it by creating romantic dinners at home, complete with candlelight and soft music. We adapted to our new way of life, and even though it was different from what we were used to, it brought us closer than ever before. We learned to appreciate every moment, every breath, every kiss, and every embrace. Our love was unshakeable, and nothing, not even a pandemic, could dampen its flame. We emerged stronger, wiser, and more in love than ever before.

When Anthony Jr told us that he wanted to put his college plans on hold to explore his passion for fashion, we were taken aback. We knew how much his scholarship meant to him and all the demanding work he has done, but we also knew that we could not stifle his dreams. We had many discussions with him, asking numerous questions to ensure that he had carefully considered his decision to pursue his passion for fashion, knowing that giving up his full scholarship was a significant choice. However, we knew how important it was to support our children's dreams and passions. Covid had taught us that life was too short to ignore our dreams and ambitions, and we wanted our son to be happy and fulfilled. So, we stood by him every step of the way, even when it was not easy.

As we adjusted to the new normal of online learning and working from home, we realized how important it was to balance work with self-care and quality time with loved ones. Brianna and Courtney went back to work, but we all remained mindful of the importance of cherishing the little moments.

Covid may have thrown us a curveball, but we were determined to make the most of it and come out stronger on the other side. It prompted us to reflect on what truly matters in life and encouraged us to pursue our dreams and passions with renewed vigor. We also learned to cherish the simple things in life and to rely on each other for support during tough times. I am grateful for the strength, resilience, and perseverance that carried us through this challenging time. While the pandemic has forever changed our lives, it has also taught us the value of unity, compassion, and the importance of cherishing the simple joys in life.

Retirement 2020

August 2020 marked the end of an era for our family, as we celebrated my husband Tony's retirement ceremony from the military. It was a momentous occasion for us, as Tony had given twenty-two and a half years of dedicated service to his country. The ceremony was a beautiful affair, with military officials, friends, and family in attendance. As Tony retired as a Master Sergeant (E-8), I was honored to be a part of his journey, standing by his side through every deployment, every move, and achievement. I could not help but feel an overwhelming sense of pride and gratitude for all that he had accomplished, sacrificed, and achieved in his career.

As we reflected on Tony's career, I could not help but think of all the times we had moved around the country, sometimes with very little notice. We always found a way to make a home wherever we went. We grew as individuals and as a couple, learning to lean on each other and support each other through thick and thin. It was not always easy, but we faced each challenge head-on, and our bond grew stronger as a result.

As Tony's official retirement date finally arrived on October 31, 2020, he had a few months of well-deserved leave to enjoy. During this time, he finally got to relax and do the things he had been putting off for so long. He slept in, went fishing on his boat frequently, and simply enjoyed the freedom of not having to worry about work for the first time in years. I could see the weight that had been on his shoulders for so long start to lift. He was finally stress-free and happy.

As a result, Tony became so much more attentive to our relationship. For the first time in a long time, I felt like he was putting our relationship first. It was like a breath of fresh air. I was grateful to see how much he had grown and changed over the years, and how much our love had grown with him. As we moved into this next chapter of our lives together, I knew that we would continue to cherish and support each other every step of the way, and that our love would only continue to grow stronger with each passing day.

As the winter months rolled in, Tony's retirement bliss started to wear off and he began to feel the itch to do something more. I could tell that he was getting restless, eager to take on a new challenge. That is when he came to me with an announcement: he wanted to go back to work and get his master's degree. I was thrilled to hear that he was ready to take on new challenges, and I knew that he would excel at whatever he put his mind to. It was inspiring to see how he always wanted to better himself and learn new things.

Tony and I always shared a deep passion for travel and adventure. We would often spend hours discussing our bucket list destinations, the foods we wanted to try, and the sights we wanted to see. And now, with this new chapter of our lives beginning, we had the chance to finally make those dreams a reality. We were ready to hit the road and experience all the world had to offer, just the two of us.

I could feel my heart race with excitement as I thought about all the new adventures that awaited us. We were both eager to create unforgettable memories and try new things together. As we moved forward into this new chapter of our lives, I knew that whatever challenges came our way, we would face them together with love and determination. For Tony and me, life was all about experiencing new things, creating lasting memories, and cherishing the bond that we had built over the years. I could not wait to see where this new adventure would take us.

Life After the Marines

Tony's dedication and hard work did not end after his military service. In fact, he went on to graduate with his master's degree, and we could not have been prouder. He continued to pursue his goals and show our children that with hard work and determination, anything is possible. His relentless pursuit of excellence was an inspiration to us all, and he always made it look so effortless. He showed us that no matter how many accomplishments we achieve, there is always room to grow, learn, and experience new things.

Despite his many achievements, Tony never lost sight of the simple pleasures in life. He continued to fish, hunt, garden, woodwork, and officiate football, and he always did it with a passion and enthusiasm that was infectious. After retiring, we traveled extensively, visiting places like Myrtle Beach, Tampa, Savannah, Atlantic Beach, Atlanta, St. Louis, and of course, Cincinnati. Together, we made so many beautiful memories that we will cherish forever.

There is nothing quite like experiencing unfamiliar places and cultures with the ones you love. It reminds us of the boundless possibilities that life has to offer and fills us with a sense of adventure and wonder. Tony's unwavering commitment to his dreams and his family serves as a reminder that anything is possible when we stay focused and determined. May we all be inspired by his example and embrace the joys of life.

As the sun rises on a new day, I am filled with gratitude for the life I'm living. After years of teaching, I took a leap of faith and made the brave decision to quit my job and focus on the things that truly mattered to me. Now, I wake up each day feeling free to explore my passions, whether that means writing, planning fun activities for my family, or shopping and making crafts.

Being at home has been a transformative experience for me, allowing me to grow and learn new things about myself every day. I have rediscovered the simple pleasures of life, like taking naps whenever I feel like it and having the time to enjoy a cup of tea in the middle of the day. The greatest gift of this new chapter of my life has been the opportunity to travel and create unforgettable memories with my family.

As a forty-six-year-old, I am grateful for this newfound freedom and excited to see what the future holds. I cannot wait to become a grandmother and share all the fun things I have discovered with my future grandchildren. I am filled with a sense of wonder and adventure as I explore the world with my family, trying new foods, and visiting exciting destinations. Life is a precious gift, and I am determined to make the most of it.

Tony's post-retirement work journey was filled with ups and downs. Although he tried out a few jobs after retiring, he finally landed a high-paying job that seemed promising, but the toxic environment and the demanding nature of the work eventually took a toll on him. For almost two years, he continued to work there, feeling unhappy and stressed, until he realized that his mental health and well-being were far more important than money. He bravely made the decision to quit just before Christmas, which turned out to be the best thing for him.

Despite the uncertainty that came with quitting, Tony knew that he deserved better and was determined to find a job that would allow him to thrive. He spent three months searching for the perfect opportunity and eventually found a job where he feels appreciated, valued, and respected. The newfound joy in his work is palpable and he could not be happier.

I am grateful that Tony continues to work while I get to retire and explore my passions. It is a testament to the kind of person Tony has become. He puts me first and is thankful for my support over the years, and now it is his turn to support me. I admire his strength, resilience, and willingness to prioritize his happiness over financial gain. Tony is an inspiration to us all, and I am proud to call him my husband.

I feel truly blessed to be able to explore my passions and spend quality time with Tony and rediscover the joys of life together. We've both been reminded that life is short and that the greatest adventures often begin with a single leap of faith. By embracing our passions and following our hearts, we can create a life filled with meaning and purpose. And who knows, perhaps the best is yet to come.

Our Adult Children

As a parent, seeing your children grow and thrive is one of the greatest joys in life. I am grateful to say that all our children have continued to flourish in their early adulthood. They have each become wonderful and talented human beings, pursuing their passions, and making a positive impact on the world around them.

Tony and I are incredibly proud of all that they have accomplished, and we feel so blessed to have a family like ours. It is a privilege to watch them grow into the best versions of themselves and to support them along the way. We cannot wait to see what the future holds for each of them, and we will always be there to cheer them on.

I am constantly in awe of Brianna's courage and determination. She has taken a leap of faith and started a new chapter of her life by moving into her first apartment in Richmond, VA, where she is following her passions for real estate and cosmetology. Brianna's creativity and eye for design have been incredibly valuable in her work, particularly when it comes to home interiors. I feel so proud to see her doing what she loves and excelling at it.

Despite her busy schedule, Brianna always is available for the people and things she loves. Her furry companion, Jesse, holds a special place in her heart, and she takes him on fun-filled adventures whenever she can. Brianna's thirst for new experiences has taken her to many beautiful places, and each one has inspired her creativity and sense of wonder.

What I admire most about Brianna is her unwavering positivity and kindness. She has a natural talent for being a cheerleader, always encouraging and uplifting those around her. Her compassion and thoughtfulness are a true testament to the beautiful soul she is. As her mother and friend, I feel so blessed to have Brianna in my life. Together, we share laughter, love, and countless memories that we will cherish forever.

Kayla is an amazing human being, and I am constantly inspired by her resilience and kind heart. As she navigates the bustling city of New York City with her two adorable pups, she pours her heart and soul into her job as a nanny for a young family. Her natural maternal instincts and caring nature make her an exceptional caregiver, and I am confident that she will make a wonderful mother someday.

Kayla's intelligence and independence are matched only by her ambition and drive. She works tirelessly as an x-ray technician during the nights, always striving to achieve her goals. Her adventurous spirit has taken her across the globe, exploring new cultures and places fearlessly, even on her own.

What truly sets Kayla apart is her unwavering loyalty and thoughtfulness. She is a loyal friend, always there to support and encourage those around her. Her infectious smile and big heart light up any room she enters. Even when things get tough, Kayla never gives up, and her fighting spirit is a true testament to the incredible person she is.

I am proud to call Kayla my daughter and my friend. Her resilience, intelligence, and kind heart inspire me every day, and I feel incredibly lucky to know and love her. Together, we have shared so many incredible memories, from exploring new cities to trying new foods. I cannot wait to see all the amazing things Kayla will accomplish in the future.

Courtney is my calm and chill daughter, and she is one of the most amazing people I know. She is not just a dental assistant; she is a force of nature. Her hardworking nature is matched only by her adventurous spirit, and she is always ready to try new things, explore new places and find new adventures. She is the kind of person who loves to do puzzles and play board games, but she also loves to fish and be outdoors. Nothing fazes her; she just lets things roll off her back, and she always keeps a level head, quick to offer good advice to those in need.

Then Eric came into her life, and everything changed. They spent all their time together, traveling and exploring unfamiliar places. They fell in love, and within two years, they were living together, engaged, and married. Watching them together is like watching a romantic movie come to life. Eric is a sweet guy who reminds me a lot of myself, and Courtney is a lot like her father. They are the perfect match for each other, and I am so happy that they found each other.

I am so proud of Courtney for being such an inspiration to all those around her. She shows us that with hard work, a positive attitude, and a sense of adventure, anything is possible. She is not just my daughter, but also my friend, and I feel so blessed to have her in my life. Watching her grow into the amazing woman she is today has been a true joy, and I cannot wait to see all the incredible things she and Eric will accomplish together.

Anthony Jr's move to New York City was the start of my son's incredible journey. With a passion for fashion and sustainability, he enrolled in fashion school, where he honed his skills and learned everything he needed to know about the industry. Soon after, he landed a job with a new streetwear clothing company that was making waves in the industry. Not only did the company sell and create unique and trendy clothing, but it also managed other creators and produced amazing social media content.

After a year of attending fashion school, he left there to pursue his work full time at the streetwear clothing company. Anthony Jr quickly moved up the ranks and became Project Manager, a testament to his hard work, creativity, and expertise. He has a gift for meeting new people, and he has never met a stranger. His charm and humor have won the hearts of everyone he meets, and he is the smartest and funniest person you will ever come across. No one can make you laugh like he can, and he is always there to share his knowledge and offer advice.

Anthony Jr has the most confidence and knowledge of anyone I know. He knows everything about everything, and he is never afraid to take risks and dream big. He is an inspiration to everyone around him, and I am so proud of him. As his mother, I am grateful to God for giving me a son like him. He has taught me so much, and I learn something new from him every day. Watching him go after his dreams and succeed has been an incredible journey, and I cannot wait to see what the future holds for him.

Life is a journey full of twists and turns, and as I look back on the past twenty-nine years, my heart overflows with joy. It has been a rollercoaster ride filled with difficulties, but I would not trade it for anything in the world. Each experience has shaped me into the person I am today, and I am grateful for every one of them.

One of the most fulfilling parts of my life has been my relationship with my husband, Tony. We have been best friends for as long as I can remember, and it has been amazing growing old together. Life is so much easier when you have someone to share it with, and Tony has been my rock through every trial and triumph.

Being a mother is an indescribable experience that fills my life with endless love, joy, and meaning. Our lives have revolved around our family, and we would not have it any other way. Our children mean everything to us, and we have cherished every moment we have spent with them. As they have grown into adults with their own lives and responsibilities, it has been challenging to get everyone together in one place. When we do, the love and laughter that fill the room is simply magical.

The memories we have created together are priceless, and I am grateful that Tony and I put in the hard work and stuck it out, never giving up on each other. We have grown and learned together, and now we are more in love than ever before. The future may be unknown, but I am ready face it head on, with excitement and anticipation for what is to come.

Our Marriage

Marriage is a journey that is full of unpredictability, and Tony and I have certainly experienced the full range of emotions that come with it. From the excitement of our wedding day to the struggles of raising children and pursuing our individual passions, we have learned that the work of maintaining a healthy and loving relationship is ongoing.

Despite the challenges that we have faced, we have come to appreciate the beauty of persistence. Even during moments of frustration, when we have taken each other for granted or allowed distance to grow between us, we have always found ways to reconnect and reignite our love. We have discovered that the key to a successful marriage is not only being able to weather the storms but also to celebrate the moments of joy and happiness together.

There have been times when Tony's hobbies, such as football or fishing, have taken priority over our relationship, and I have felt like we were drifting apart. Similarly, there have been moments when we have become complacent and felt more like roommates than lovers. However, we have always persevered, never giving up on each other.

Communication has been crucial in our journey, and we have learned to truly listen and understand each other's needs. By doing so, we have grown individually and as a couple. We have discovered that love requires continuous effort and dedication, and we have been willing to put in the work to maintain our relationship.

Looking back, it is inspiring to know that no matter what obstacles we have faced, our love has never faltered. We have learned that a successful marriage is not about avoiding the tough times but rather about persevering through them together. It is this commitment to each other that has brought us to where we are today, stronger, and more in love than ever before.

Our journey as a couple has not been without its share of difficulties, but throughout it all, the connection between Tony and I remained strong and passionate. Our chemistry is undeniable, and our physical intimacy was a priority for us from the very beginning. We shared a deep and electric bond that only grew stronger with time.

Even when we faced our toughest challenges, we always found comfort and solace in each other's arms. The passion that we shared was a lifeline that kept us connected, even when we struggled to communicate in other areas of our relationship. While we certainly faced differences in our sex drives at different points in our relationship, the intimacy that we shared was always incredible.

In hindsight, I realized that I craved that physical connection so intensely because it was the one time when Tony gave me his full attention and affection. Though he may not have shown much emotion in our day-to-day life, when we were together physically, he let his guard down and I felt truly seen and loved. Our physical connection was a reminder that, despite our differences and difficulties, we were still in love and committed to each other.

Navigating differences in sex drive can be a challenging aspect of any relationship, but over time Tony and I have learned to find a balance that works for both of us. Tony made a conscious effort to prioritize his mental health and learned to let go of stress, which allowed him to be more present and affectionate in our daily life. As a result, our physical connection has become stronger than ever before, and we feel like teenagers again.

We have come to realize that physical intimacy is not just about the act itself, but also about the deep emotional connection that it fosters between us. It is a reminder that we are still in love and committed to each other, even after all these years.

We are grateful for this aspect of our relationship and see it as a constant source of inspiration and love. We made a conscious effort to keep the romance alive, and now we are enjoying a newfound excitement in our intimate life. It just goes to show that no matter how long you have been with someone, with effort and understanding, you can keep the flame burning bright.

It was a revelation when I realized that taking care of myself was not selfish, but necessary for my own well-being and for my family. I always put everyone before myself. I supported everyone around me, and I never had energy left for me. I was forty years old, and I did not even know what I liked to do or who I was besides a wife and mother.

Tony also had to go through a similar journey of self-discovery and self-love. We both started pursuing our passions and interests, taking time to do things that brought us joy and fulfillment. We started to appreciate ourselves more and that reflected in our relationship as well. We were no longer just spouses, but also best friends who supported and encouraged each other to be the best version of ourselves. We were able to rediscover ourselves and fall in love all over again. It was like a second chance at life, and we were not going to waste it.

Learning to communicate effectively can be a significant challenge in any relationship. Tony and I were no exception to this, and it was something we struggled with early on in our marriage. However, we both realized that without open and honest communication, our relationship would not survive. So, we made a conscious effort to work on our communication skills.

Through a lot of trial and error, Tony learned to listen without becoming defensive, and I learned to express myself in a way that was both honest and constructive. It was not always easy, and we had our fair share of disagreements, but we never gave up on each other. As we continued to practice these skills, we noticed a significant shift in our relationship. We became more connected and began to understand each other on a much deeper level.

Today, we make it a priority to check in with each other regularly and discuss any concerns or feelings that may arise. It is a beautiful thing to know that we can truly be vulnerable with each other and grow together as individuals and as a couple. Our ability to communicate openly and honestly has become the foundation of our relationship and has allowed us to create a bond that is unbreakable.

It is often said that opposites attract, and that was certainly true for Tony and me. However, it was not until we started working together on projects that we realized just how different we were. It was like we were from different planets. Tony was a big-picture thinker, with an eye for detail and an analytical mind. I, on the other hand, was more intuitive and creative, with a knack for finding new solutions to problems. At first, our differences caused friction, and we struggled to find common ground. Over time, we learned to appreciate each other's unique perspectives and talents.

Instead of seeing our differences as a source of conflict, we began to see them as a strength. We learned to communicate more effectively, using a combination of visuals and verbal explanations to ensure we were both on the same page. We also learned to be more patient with each other, recognizing that our diverse ways of thinking and processing information were not flaws to be fixed, but rather opportunities for growth and learning.

As we worked together on various projects, we discovered that our partnership had grown stronger and more resilient. We became better equipped to face life's challenges together, knowing that we could rely on each other's strengths to overcome any obstacles. Our ability to work together and appreciate each other's differences not only strengthened our relationship but also helped us succeed in our careers and other areas of our lives.

When it comes to our differences in dealing with stress, it took time for me and Tony to understand and appreciate each other's approach. I used to get frustrated when Tony would push me to talk about things when I needed space, but I came to realize that we just wanted to help and find a solution. Over time, Tony learned that when I needed space, it was not a rejection of him, but rather a way for me to process my thoughts and feelings.

What is utterly amazing is that even when we are not on the same page, we still have this unbreakable bond. We know that we are in this together and that we can always rely on each other. Our love has grown stronger with each challenge we have faced and each difference we have overcome. We inspire each other to be our best selves and we lift each other up when we fall. We always remember that it is not about winning an argument or debate, but that we are one team, one fight. When Tony wins, I win, our family wins.

Love Languages

Learning about our love languages was a complete game-changer in our relationship. We stumbled upon Gary Chapman's book, "*Five Love Languages*," and it opened our eyes to a whole new level of understanding one another. We discovered that the way we express and receive love can be vastly different, and that realization helped us overcome misunderstandings and unfulfilled expectations.

The five love languages - physical touch, receiving gifts, acts of service, quality time, and words of affirmation - allowed us to understand each other on a deeper level. We learned that it was not just about knowing our own love language, but also about understanding and speaking our partner's language. Over time, we realized that our love languages could change, and that being attuned to those changes was vital to the health and happiness of our relationship.

Initially, I struggled to understand Tony's love language, which was receiving gifts, while mine was quality time/acts of service. I would plan grand dates and adventures, but he did not seem to enjoy them as much as I did. On the other hand, when Tony would surprise me with presents, I would sometimes react negatively, being ungrateful and distant. Despite his efforts, I did not feel fulfilled, and I longed for more intimate moments with just the two of us.

It was only when we started speaking each other's language that we could see the sparks reigniting. I began to see the romance in Tony's gifts, and he found meaning in my acts of service and quality time. It was a beautiful realization that strengthened our bond and brought us closer together.

As I paid closer attention to Tony's actions, I realized that he expressed his love by doing things for me that I needed and wanted. He would build furniture pieces for our home, scratch my head and back every night, and even go grocery shopping with me. He would surprise me with my favorite snacks and hold my hand as we watched a movie. These small, everyday moments were how he showed his love for me, and I learned to appreciate them even more than grand romantic gestures.

Today, I still love planning extravagant trips and romantic nights, and Tony is fully supportive of me doing so. I have also come to appreciate the little things that make our everyday life special. We have come to realize that all those little everyday moments are what truly matter in our relationship, and we cherish them dearly.

Us As Individuals

A healthy relationship is not only about being together but also about allowing each other to grow individually. It is essential to have personal interests, hobbies, and passions that give you a sense of fulfillment and purpose. Engaging in activities that make you happy outside of your relationship can provide a sense of balance and prevent feelings of being suffocated or restricted in the partnership.

Having space for your hobbies can also help you relax and recharge, which can ultimately benefit your relationship. For instance, taking a painting class, joining a book club, or playing a sport can be a healthy way to relieve stress and improve your mood. Engaging in these activities can bring positive energy into the relationship.

However, it is crucial to be mindful of how much time and energy you spend on your hobbies and interests. It is essential not to let your activities consume you or take priority over your partner's needs and wants. Striking a balance between work, hobbies, kids, and spouse can be challenging, but it is necessary to keep the relationship strong and healthy.

When you prioritize your partner's needs and wants, you demonstrate that they are important to you. Even when life gets busy, it is crucial to be available for your partner. Trying to be present and attentive to your partner's needs can go a long way in keeping the relationship healthy.

Remember that you are your own person, and maintaining your individuality can be empowering and strengthen the bond between you and your partner. When you are confident in yourself and your interests, you bring more depth and richness to the relationship. So, make sure to take time for yourself while also being mindful of your partner's needs and wants. It can help you to grow as individuals and strengthen your relationship as a couple.

As we delved deeper into each other's passions and interests, our love story grew more vibrant and captivating each day. The mere sight of Tony pouring his soul into creating stunning woodwork pieces would set my heart aflutter. His culinary prowess, as he expertly grilled and cooked up delicious meals for us, made me feel adored and cherished in every sense.

It was not just the grand gestures that made our love story special - it was the everyday moments that we shared. From snuggling up together to watch a movie to discovering new things together, every moment spent with Tony felt like a new adventure. Even the simplest of gestures, like his gentle touch as he brushed my hair away from my face or the way he held my hand while strolling through the park, ignited a passionate romance that left me breathless.

What truly made our relationship extraordinary was the unwavering support we provided each other to chase our dreams and reach our aspirations. Tony empowered me to pursue my passions with unwavering determination and never gave up on me, even in the face of doubt.

The beauty of our relationship was not only found in the love we shared, but also in the unwavering support we offered each other in pursuing our wildest dreams and aspirations. Tony was my biggest cheerleader, motivating me to pursue my passions with unrelenting determination, even in the face of self-doubt. His unwavering support and belief in me allowed me to flourish and grow into the best version of myself. I did the same for him, pushing him to explore his passions and chase the things that brought him happiness and joy.

Our relationship taught me that love goes beyond material gifts and grand gestures. It is about being there for each other through the highs and lows, the good and the bad. It is about celebrating each other's victories and picking each other up when we fall. Most importantly, it is about cherishing the little moments and finding romance in the everyday moments we share together. Whether it is a lazy Sunday spent cuddled up together, or an impromptu adventure exploring new sights, every moment spent with Tony was filled with love and enchantment. Our love story has taught me that true love is about supporting each other, growing together, and creating memories that will last a lifetime.

Our relationship is a testament to the power of individuality and resilience. We took the time to discover who we are as individuals, and it has only strengthened our bond as a couple. Tony's love for football, fishing, gardening, and the great outdoors is nothing short of inspiring. Seeing him thrive in his element out on the water or in the woods is a remarkable sight. What is even more enchanting is his skill with his hands. Whether it is fixing our car or creating a stunning piece of furniture, his passion for craftsmanship is unmatched. And let us not forget about his culinary talents - his love for cooking and experimenting with new recipes never ceases to keep our taste buds on their toes.

What truly sets Tony apart is his devotion to our family. His unwavering dedication and willingness to do anything for us is simply awe-inspiring. Seeing him love and cherish our family with such fervor fills my heart with an indescribable joy. I am beyond grateful to have him as my partner and to be a part of this incredible journey we call life. Our relationship has taught me that true love is about accepting each other for who we are, supporting each other through our passions, and being there for each other through thick and thin.

For me, it has been a journey to discover my passions, but now that I have, I feel more encouraged than ever before. Family time is at the top of my list, and I try to make every moment count with my loved ones. I adore creating thoughtful gifts that show my family how much I care, planning fun parties and creating an atmosphere of joy and togetherness. I get excited about coming up with new games to play during family game night, and I love making the holidays special with unique and memorable activities. I even dress up in festive attire to show my love for the season.

Expressing myself through makeup and beauty products brings me joy and helps me enhance my natural beauty. Planning romantic date nights at home is another way I connect with my partner, creating a cozy and intimate environment that brings us closer. I love celebrating birthdays, decorating, and making my loved ones feel special and appreciated. Singing and listening to music fills me with inspiration and motivation, and I adore being silly and letting loose with my family during karaoke nights.

My creativity shines when I make crafts and teach, bringing joy and learning to others. Cooking and trying out new recipes bring everyone together. I take pride in keeping my home clean and organized, which gives me a sense of control and accomplishment. More than anything, being a mother is my calling, and it inspires me every day to be the best version of myself.

Life Lessons

Looking back on our life together, I am amazed at how far we have come as a couple. Tony and I used to be so fragile and selfish, with no understanding of what it meant to have a healthy relationship. Our disagreements were like explosions, leaving behind a trail of hurt feelings and misunderstandings. I used to believe that I always had to be in control, and Tony would often retreat into silence to avoid confrontation. It was a vicious cycle that left us both feeling drained and disconnected.

Over time, we have learned how to communicate more effectively. We no longer fight to win, but instead strive to understand each other's perspectives. We listen actively and empathize with each other's feelings. We have learned to compromise and find solutions that benefit us both. It has been a long and challenging road, but the rewards have been well worth it.

Now, as empty nesters, we finally have the time and freedom to pursue our passions and make the most of each day. We love spending time together, whether we are exploring new places, cooking a delicious meal together, or simply lounging on the porch swing, savoring the warmth of the sun. We also love singing and listening to music together, and we often have impromptu dance parties in the living room.

Despite all our differences, Tony and I are a true dream team. We have overcome countless obstacles to get to this point, and our bond has only grown stronger as a result. Home is our sanctuary, a place of peace and comfort where we can simply be ourselves. I am excited to see what the future holds for us and can't wait to continue exploring all the joys and adventures life has to offer together.

Our Family

As a family, Tony and I have always believed in the power of experiences over material possessions. Instead of spending all our money on flashy gadgets or luxury items, we have chosen to prioritize quality time with each other. While we may not have been able to afford fancy vacations or jet-set around the world, we found ways to create special moments right at home. From impromptu dance parties to family game nights, we made sure to carve out time for each other and bond over the things we love.

One of our favorite family traditions is having cookouts and barbecues in our backyard. We spend hours prepping the food and setting up the grill, creating an atmosphere of excitement and anticipation. As the food sizzled on the grill, we would play games, tell stories, listen to music, and just enjoy each other's company. It was the perfect way to unwind and connect after a long week.

Another way we made memories was through surprise parties and birthdays for our family. We would spend weeks planning the perfect celebration, from decorations to the menu. On the day of the party, we would watch as the guest of honor walked into a room filled with love and laughter. Seeing the joy on their faces was priceless and made all the effort worth it.

Most importantly, we made sure to teach our children the value of experiences over material possessions. We wanted them to know that memories can last a lifetime, while material things can be lost or forgotten. We hope that the memories we created as a family will stay with them and inspire them to prioritize the people they love above all else.

There is nothing sexier than a man who loves and supports his children, and my husband Tony embodies that in every way. His devotion to being a great father is not only admirable, but it is also inspiring. Watching him interact with our children fills me with such pride and joy.

As a father, Tony wears many hats - he is a coach, a cheerleader, a wise counsel, a friend, and a teacher. He is there for our children no matter what, whether it is at school, church, or any other event. His unwavering support and encouragement have helped our children learn valuable life lessons, such as the importance of hard work, dedication, and perseverance. Tony has even passed down his love for football, particularly his passion for the Cincinnati Bengals. Above all, he has taught our kids to be kind, honest, compassionate, and always willing to help those in need.

What makes Tony's dedication to our family even more special is that he never had a positive father figure in his own life. Yet, he has gone above and beyond to give our children everything he never had, and for that, I am forever grateful. He has created a home filled with love, support, and understanding, where our children feel safe and happy. He has shown our children how to love deeply and unconditionally, and that is a lesson that they will carry with them for the rest of their lives.

Tony's commitment to our family does not stop there. He also manages to balance his career and our marriage while making sure he has time for our children. Even when his schedule is hectic, he always finds a way to be there for them. He listens to their problems and offers guidance and support. He is always there to celebrate their accomplishments, no matter how small.

Watching Tony be such a devoted father and husband is one of the greatest joys of my life. It is a reminder that, with love and dedication, anything is possible.

Tony's unwavering dedication to our family has been a driving force in creating a strong and loving household. His constant presence and commitment to being a supportive and involved father have inspired our children to emulate his example and cherish the value of family. He has instilled in them the importance of being present and actively showing love and care to the people they hold dear. I have no doubt that his role as a father has played a crucial role in shaping the person our children have become.

As a family, we have created a home filled with love, laughter, and support. We have always encouraged our children to pursue their dreams and passions, no matter how big or small. We have also taught them to embrace their mistakes and learn from them, allowing them to grow and become better people. We have been transparent about our past struggles, sharing our experiences with financial difficulties and drug use. This openness has allowed us to build trust and teach our children valuable lessons that they can apply to their own lives.

As parents, Tony and I believe that our children need more than just practical skills to live a successful life; they also need emotional skills to lead a fulfilling one. We hope to instill in them the importance of effective communication, honesty, and expressing their feelings. We want them to understand the beauty of being vulnerable and the power of taking care of themselves and others.

Our love story is something we want our children to be inspired by. We hope to show them that a relationship built on love, respect, and passion is possible. We believe in the little things, like holding hands and stealing kisses, and that true love requires work, patience, and compromise.

We also want our children to inherit our thirst for adventure and passion for life. We encourage them to pursue their dreams and explore the world without fear. Our hope is that they will continue to grow into compassionate, independent, and adventurous adults who make a positive impact in the world.

Tony and I have learned so much from each other and are inspired every day by the love we share. We are fully committed to our family and each other, mind, body, and soul. We have built a life that brings us joy and fulfillment, and we hope to impart this wisdom to our children. We believe in them, and we know that nothing can stop them from achieving their dreams.

The Journey

In this beautiful journey called life, there will always be challenges and setbacks that test us. But amidst the chaos and uncertainty, we must keep moving forward and never give up on ourselves. For it is in those moments of struggle that we learn and grow the most. When we are fortunate enough to share this journey with someone special, love becomes our guiding light, giving us the courage to overcome any obstacle. With the right person by our side, we can face any challenge with confidence and rise above our limitations. Let us hold on to the hope that each setback brings new opportunities for us to grow, both as individuals and as partners. For in the end, the greatest triumphs are those that we achieve with the ones we love.

Remember, life is a beautiful journey of constant evolution, and change is inevitable. It may be difficult at times, but trust that things will get better. When you are lucky enough to share this journey with someone special, their love and support can be the anchor that keeps you grounded amidst the winds of change. Believe in yourself and have faith that you can overcome any obstacle, for with the right mindset and the right person by your side, anything is possible. Let the challenges of life be the catalysts that transform you into the best version of yourself, both individually and together as a couple. Embrace the changes that come your way, for they hold within them the seeds of new opportunities and greater happiness. Keep the flame of love burning bright, and let it be the light that guides you through even the darkest of days.

It is okay to ask for help when we need it. In fact, it takes great courage and strength to admit our vulnerabilities and seek support from others. Let us not be too proud to lean on our loved ones for support and guidance. Together, we can create a community of forgiveness, kindness, honesty, and compassion, where everyone feels valued and supported. When we share our struggles and triumphs with those we love, we deepen our bonds and create a sense of belonging that can sustain us through even the toughest times. Let us be a beacon of hope and inspiration to others by living with kindness and compassion in our hearts. For it is through our collective efforts that we can make the world a better place, one small act of kindness at a time. As we journey through life, let us hold on to the love and support of those who lift us up and inspire us to be our best selves.

We are all unique individuals with our own beautiful story to tell. Embrace who you are, and do not let anyone dim your light. You are here for a reason, and your unique gifts and talents are needed in this world. Share your journey with the world, inspire others to do the same, and always keep pushing forward, no matter how difficult the road may seem. When you stay true to yourself and live authentically, you inspire others to do the same, and that's when magic happens. Let your light shine bright, and let the world bask in the radiance of your spirit. When we embrace our individuality and celebrate our differences, we create a tapestry of beauty and diversity that enriches us all. So, never be afraid to be who you truly are, and never let anyone dull your sparkle. You are a shining star, and the world is waiting to be dazzled by your brilliance.

Building a Stronger Family and a Better World

Our family is built on a solid foundation of love and empathy that has brought us closer together and made us a team. We have learned the value of faith in our lives, which has provided us with guidance, purpose, and a belief in a higher power that gives us strength and direction. It has taught us to extend love and forgiveness to ourselves and others, allowing us to heal from emotional wounds, let go of resentment and anger, and move past mistakes. This has strengthened our family bonds and brought us closer together, creating an unbreakable bond of love and support that helps us navigate through life's challenges.

The Circle of Redemption is a reminder that we should live with kindness, compassion, and forgiveness, using these virtues as tools to build stronger communities, promote equality and justice, and foster understanding and empathy across cultures and backgrounds. We are all called to create a more just, loving, and compassionate world, one that celebrates diversity and recognizes the value of every human being.

By coming together in love and faith, we can work towards this vision, creating a world where everyone can thrive and live a life of purpose and meaning. Let us embrace the Circle of Redemption and use it as a guide to build a brighter future for ourselves and our loved ones.